Endorsem...

"Kim Brooks' love for God's Word and for men and women of God is apparent in her latest work. She has painstakingly collected sound advice that can be a guide to all who seek not only God's way of dating but the most successful way. If you read this book, and apply its words, you will have the skills you need to find love without the heartache, games, and drama sagas."

-CHRISTINE PEMBLETON, marriage expert and author of,
Lord, I'm Ready To Be a Wife

"This is a book that will grab your attention, challenge your motives, and move you to reach for the expectations of God in finding the right relationship."

-PASTOR LOUIS SMITH, author of bestseller,
Sexual Sins of the Bible on, *He's Fine...But is He Saved?*

"Kim's ministry to singles is sprinkled with a blend of the unadulterated Word of God, realism, humor and love. If you plan to hear her minister, then prepare to be changed!"

-TIA McCOLLORS, author of inspirational novels,
The Truth About Love, Zora's Cry, and
A Heart of Devotion

"Kim Brooks is a very experienced speaker, and she did an excellent job of delivering a powerful message at our prayer breakfast conference earlier this year. Her versatile and very upbeat message kept us enthralled the whole time and she was 'encored for more' when she was done. Her unique blend of passion, humor, and sincerity makes her highly recommended. She knew her material well, but also left herself open to be innovative and move to the rhythm of the audience. We were impressed with her incredible gift of impact, and I can honestly say she's one of the best keynotes we've ever had and we look forward to having her come and speak for us again in the near future."

-JUDITH CLARK, Executive Director Women Who Care Ministries, Inc. Gaithersburg, MD

"I've watched Kim . . . I have seen very few people as dedicated to her dream as she has been. Kim is a gifted writer. Her style of writing draws you in and keeps you engaged."

-REBECCA OSAIGBOVO, author of
Chosen Vessels and *It's Not About You -It's About God*

"Kim Brooks brings her mastery of writing to the non-fictional topic of dating, where she grabs you by the hand and delves into the true elements of Christian dating from a biblical perspective sliced with her own personal triumphs and challenges. Kim awakens the reader to the heart of God and to the true meaning of Christian dating."

-ED HOUSTON, Author of *Single and Living Free*

"When my wife and I dated, God abstained us from having premarital sex. If one really believes that the person they are about to marry is precious in God's sight, then honor that man or woman of God and keep yourself pure before marriage... I knew my wife was the one for me so I didn't want to disrespect God or my wife's body so we waited for marriage. I am so glad we waited!"

-SHON HYNEMAN author of,
It's The Woman You Gave Me

Blessings!

HOW TO DATE AND STAY SAVED

by Bestselling Author

KIM BROOKS

Driven Enterprises, LLC Detroit, Michigan

How to Date and Stay Saved
© 2010 Kimberley Brooks

ISBN: 978-0-9760390-4-4
Library of Congress Control No. 2010920213

Driven Enterprises, LLC
P.O. Box 231856
Detroit, MI 48223

Visit our website www.DateAndStaySaved.com

Cover Design and Interior Layout: LaTanya Orr
www.iselah.com
Editor: Skyla P. Thomas of Pleasant Words, LLC
www.PleasantWords.net

Cover Photos: Stage4fotografik
Cover Makeup Artist: Jessica Y. Hernandez

All Scripture quotations, unless noted otherwise, are taken
From The Holy Bible, King James Version

Printed in the United States of America.

*Thy word have I hid
in mine heart,
that I might not sin
against thee.*

-Psalm 119:11

TABLE OF CONTENTS

Introduction

A contemporary gospel artist, Canton Jones, penned a hit song entitled, "Stay Saved." It's about the daily encounters Christians may face which challenge their flesh and sometimes make them wanna slap somebody! However, the point of the song is when presented with those kinds of "opportunities" instead of yielding to the flesh, continue in the Spirit and *stay saved*, which may mean walking in love, or simply walking away.

As a believer, once you're saved and receive Jesus Christ as your personal Lord and Savior, the one thing that is evident is that you have a heart for God. You have a desire to know God, otherwise you would not have accepted His invitation of salvation. It's kinda like when you're getting married to someone, if you don't meet the groom at the altar, it may be a good indication that you don't really love him and simply want to have nothing to do with him. The same thing goes with God.

Many of us, myself included, got saved by meeting God at the altar, in the form of a salvation invitation presented by a pastor or a man or woman of God. So your heart is there. You want to do right. You want to receive God's love, and be all the man or woman

God called you to be. However, you may not know how a Christian is to operate when it comes to dating and relating with the opposite sex. It's not like you're handed a dating instruction manual once you get saved.

For the past five years I have ministered across the country on how to be victorious, content, abstinent, and drama-free single believers. One of my most popular workshops is on sex and dating. I also minister each month via email in my e-Newsletter, *The Single Heart*, which encourages, inspires, informs, and edifies thousands of single believers and is subscribable, for free, on my website *www.DateandStaySaved.com.* What I've discovered in my travels and from talking to and receiving emails from countless single saints is that many want to do right by God and be abstinent, but just don't know *how* to do it. One person asked me, "How do I remain abstinent when my hormones are raging!" That question, to me, is very honest, and very real. Just because you're saved doesn't mean your desire for sex automatically goes away.

After hearing the cries of countless singles, I decided to take most of the material I use in my workshops, along with additional revelation the Lord has given me through His Word and practical application, and place it in this book. I have poured my heart and soul into this book, and even tell on myself and share my own personal business with the sincere desire that you receive the Word, apply the Word, and be changed for the rest of your life.

No longer do you have to struggle as a single believer, feeling "less saved" because you want to "get it on" like Marvin Gaye; instead you'll learn how to date and stay saved, and how to allow God to keep you from here on out until your wedding day.

Some questions which may have been asked with regards to dating include: Is there a difference between dating before you were saved, and after you were saved? If you're used to having sex on the regular before you were saved, does God expect you to give all that up? If so, *how*, especially when your flesh is used to that desire being fulfilled? In other words, how can you date *AND* stay saved?

This book will answer all these questions and more.

The desire to please God may be in your heart, but you may not have the proper tools, knowledge and information in order to effectively carry it out. The main tool we'll be using throughout this book is the best tool, which is the Word of God. Yes, the Bible has a lot to say on the subject. The Word also says my people are destroyed for lack of knowledge *(Hosea 4:6)*, and God doesn't want us to be destroyed, so that means He wouldn't set an expectation for us and then not provide a way for that expectation to be met. His Word is the keeping power, and the instruction manual.

Within the pages of this book, I'll offer suggestions on how to be kept by God in a dating relationship. This book is not just a set of Christian dating do's and don'ts, but it's a compilation of suggestions from the Word of God and my own personal experiences which have allowed me to be kept by God my entire life. Now don't get it twisted, I'm not implying that if you have sex outside of marriage that you're not saved anymore. Thank God for the grace of God in that if we miss it and sincerely go to Him with the heart intention of not making the same mistake twice, then He said He will forgive our sin and cleanse us of all our unrighteousness *(1 John 1:9)*. However, a lot of times, when some people miss it, they say things like, "It just happened," whereas I believe that nothing, "just happens."

This book is for those of us who want to live a life as successful single saints whose lifestyle pleases God – who want to avoid temptation and who want to glorify God with our bodies. This book is for those of us who want all life has to offer, including healthy relationships and true love and happiness, without compromising our religious beliefs or hindering our fellowship with God.

The final chapter of this book concludes with Christian couples who did it – they dated for at least a year, remained abstinent the entire time they dated, and are now happily married! Some of them come from a sexually active past; some don't. Allow their testimonies to encourage and show you that it *is possible* to date someone who will love you for you and not just for what you have to offer in the bedroom – someone who has no desire to "try you out" before making a commitment to love you for a lifetime. Despite what our sex-driven society says, two people *can* meet, date, and marry without falling into sexual sin in the process.

Before we dive right in, I want to first define the word, "dating," as it will be used in this book.

When I mention, "dating," I'm not talking about casual dating, or just hanging out with someone every week that you have no intention of getting to know for the purpose of a long-term relationship. I'm not talking about "Goodtime Charlie" dating either, where you're just dating to pass time, or because you're bored and just want someone to go catch a movie with, or feel proud being seen with on your arm even though you secretly can't stand him or her. No, I'm speaking of what I call *purposeful dating.*

THE PURPOSE OF CHRISTIAN DATING

as used in this book is as follows:

*To discover, through prayer, the leading of
the Holy Spirit, and through gathering
information whether or not the person you
are consistently and exclusively dating has
the potential to be your spouse.*

So now that you understand what I mean
when I use the term "dating," let's continue
on this journey together and discover how
to date *AND* stay saved!

Chapter 1

WHAT'S LOVE GOT TO DO WITH IT?

In 1984, Tina Turner recorded a popular song which asks, "What's love got to do, got to do with it? What's love, but a second hand emotion?" Well, to answer Ms. Turner's first question, my answer is emphatically, everything! The force of love should govern everything we do, everything we say, and every decision we make. I also want to add that love isn't just a "second hand emotion," but it's an action.

God loves you so much that He sent His only begotten son, Jesus, to die on the cross in your place so that you wouldn't have to spend eternity apart from God in hell. God had you on His mind when He sent Jesus that He even said, *"Yet it pleased the Lord to bruise him; he hath put him to grief: when thou shalt make his soul an offering for sin, he shall see his seed, he shall prolong his days, and the pleasure of the Lord shall prosper in his hand"* (Isaiah 53:10). God joyfully looked on as His Son was beaten, bruised, and spat upon because He knew that Jesus' sacrifice and obedience meant that God bought you back with the price of the shed blood of Jesus Christ to have and keep you in His loving arms forever.

What does this have to do with Christian dating, you may ask?

Well, before we talk about dating relationships, which we will begin covering in the next chapter, we must first talk about the one love relationship that should be the foundation of every relationship thereafter – your relationship with God.

Everyone wants to be "in love." Everybody wants someone to love them totally and completely, and accept them for who they are and all of their flaws. Some people grow up never experiencing this kind of love in the home so they look for it in others, or in the form of a man or woman to hold them, love them, sex them up while promising to never leave them nor forsake them, only to be disappointed when after a few rolls in the hay, they stop calling or returning their phone calls.

A wise minister once said, love has to be vertical, first, before it can ever be horizontal.

Before you determine whether you're ready to date someone, you must first determine that you're in love with God, so much so that God's will and God's desires govern and guide your dating relationships.

This doesn't happen overnight.

Once you get saved, or receive Jesus Christ as your personal Lord and Savior, you become a new creature in Christ Jesus. Indeed, old things are passed away, and behold all things are become new *(2 Corinthians 5:17)*. Your spirit gets saved, but you still have to battle with the flesh.

Your spirit wants to live for God and please God, but the beast known as the flesh wants to keep doing its own thing, keep having sex -if it was enjoying it before salvation, and keep living according to the ways of the past. This is why it's so important to not only get saved, but to also mature spiritually and allow your mind to be renewed by the Word of God.

*As newborn babes, desire the sincere milk of
the word, that ye may grow thereby.*
1 Peter 2:2

*And be not conformed to this world: but be ye
transformed by the renewing of your mind, that ye
may prove what is that good, and acceptable,
and perfect, will of God.*
Romans 12:2

Your mind ultimately tells your body, or your flesh, what to do. The key is to control what you feed your mind.

What goes into your eye and ear gates determine what you think on and meditate, whether it's God's Word or the latest R. Kelly song or video.

Do you ever notice how if you go a few days without praying and then listen to the latest R & B hits and go to the show to see a romantic comedy then all of a sudden you're hornier than ever before and just want to have sex with the next fine person you see? That's because you've been feeding your flesh instead of feeding your spirit man. There is a popular saying, "Starve your doubt and feed your faith." However, I want to introduce another saying as it pertains to this book, "Starve your flesh and feed your spirit."

The more you position yourself, single believer, underneath the Word to consistently hear it and allow the Word to get ingrained in your mind, only then will you become that tree planted by the rivers of water, that will produce fruit in its season, whose leaf will not wither, and whatsoever you do shall prosper *(Psalm 1:3).*

CONSISTENCY IS KEY

Whether it's going to your local church more than just on Sundays, or spending time in the Word daily - even if it means reading and meditating one Scripture a day - the key is consistency. The more consistent you spend time with God in prayer and in His Word, the more victorious you will be as a single believer.

Not only that, but the more Word you deposit into your spirit man, the more Christ-like you will become where His desires become your desires, and your main desire changes into wanting to please God in every area of your life, including your relationships.

For it is God which worketh in you both to will
and to do of his good pleasure.
Philippians 2:13

I can remember when I decided to totally commit to God. The reason I say, "totally commit to God" is because when I first got saved at the age of eighteen at a choir concert, I just viewed my salvation as "fire insurance." You know, "I don't want to go to hell so I may as well get saved." After that, nothing changed; I kept clubbin' every other week and talking about people. Nothing changed except I felt like I wasn't going to hell anymore. Then a year later my best friend brought me to my current church home, where I heard the Word taught and preached in a way where I could actually apply it to my everyday life. Then she took me to the church's very first singles meeting for singles under 26 where I witnessed other single believers my age excitedly testify and I thought to myself, "Wow, so it *is* possible to live for God and be a young, enthusiastic single saint!" So I joined the church after visiting six months, and started attending services on Sundays, mid-week services, daily early morning prayer, and began to serve in several auxiliaries including the outreach department. I, on purpose, planted my two feet underneath the Word because I was hungry for more of God!

When I started attending my new church home regularly, I must admit, I was still clubbin' at first. I was still meeting guys at the club, exchanging phone numbers, and hookin' up with them the next weekend. However, I can remember the last time where the Holy Ghost arrested me and I said, "Enough!"

At the age of 20 I met this fine guy at a Detroit club. Even before I was saved I would never approach a guy first, but would offer quick glances. Well, it worked and the guy came over and introduced himself and we eventually exchanged numbers.

One afternoon he came by my mom's house (mom must have been upstairs or gone), and we began holding and kissing each other on the couch. I was used to making out this way with guys before, but for some reason this time felt different. I felt like I was doing something I shouldn't have been doing, and I wanted him to stop. So I told him I didn't want to continue for "spiritual reasons," however he tried to convince me that it was "okay," for two people to still have sex even though they're just friends. Now in the back of my mind I knew we weren't about to have sex. Even before I was saved I had made it up in my mind that the first person I had sex with would be someone I truly loved and not just some "friend with benefits." I politely told the guy to get up and he obliged, took a sip of red Kool-aid on the coffee table, and just looked at me. I then asked him to leave, and he did.

Once I shut the door behind him, I retreated to

the couch, fell on my knees and wept like a baby! I felt like I hurt God, and the last thing I wanted to do was disappoint my Heavenly Father. It was then that I made the decision to not have sex before marriage, because my love for God was so strong that I didn't want to hurt Him anymore.

I believe the reason my relationship with God changed from love out of fear (i.e. saved for fire insurance) to love out of conviction (i.e. saved based on a true love relationship with God) is because while I was feeding the flesh with this boy, I had been attending church regularly, hearing the Word, reading the Word, so much so that God's desires had become my desires; the light bulb had come on and God had become real to me.

We must realize, single believers, that God is a real person with real feelings and real desires for you and me. No, He's not just some judge up in heaven ready to strike you down the first time you make a mistake. He's a merciful God, a forgiving God, and a patient God, and He's just waiting for you to give your all to Him, not because He forces you to, but because you want to. God made man as a willful being. We *choose* whether or not to do right by Him.

THE BEST LOVER

God is a God of relationship. He created Adam in His own image and after His own likeness because He craved fellowship with another person like Him *(Genesis 1:26)*. God wanted someone He could walk with and talk with throughout the course of the day. His only desire was to please Adam, as God gave Adam access to everything in the garden, except the one tree in the center. He also gave Adam dominion, authority, and the ability to name the very animals God created *(Genesis 2:15-19)*.

But again, God gave mankind free will and Adam decided to go against God's boundary as He decided to partake of the forbidden fruit from the tree which was off-limits. Adam and his wife, Eve, went against God's one command and both ate the fruit anyway. God then placed a curse upon them and drove Adam and Eve out of the Garden of Eden. Man then began to multiply and became wicked in the sight of God. The Word says, *"And it repented the Lord that he had made man on the earth, and it grieved him at his heart."* *(Genesis 6:6)* The word, "repenteth" in this Scripture means, to be sorry or suffer grief.

God was sorry and saddened by the fact that the very man that He created to simply fellowship with, enjoy His company, and bless with dominion and authority, decided to turn his back on Him by becoming rebellious and wicked. God was sad because that was not his intention for mankind. He wiped out mankind one time with the flood and decided to start over, but then said He wouldn't do that again and sealed that covenant promise with a rainbow *(Genesis 9:13)*.

Instead, God sent His only begotten Son to die in our place so that even though mankind born after Adam is born with the same sinful nature that Adam had (where mankind's first inclination is to sin rather than live righteous), all we have to do is receive Jesus Christ into our hearts according to *Romans 10:8-10* and utilize God's love letter, known as the Bible, as a guide for our daily affairs and discretions.

Why would God go through all this trouble to make sure we could be free?

Why would God put up with man seemingly stabbing Him in the back, going against His will, and acting like He wasn't even there or didn't even create him in the first place?

The reason could be summed up in one word: Love.

God loved, and He did something about it.

LOVE HAS EVERYTHING TO DO WITH IT

When it comes to dating relationships, we love God, first, and how we conduct ourselves in dating relationships flows from our #1 goal to please God not just with our lips but with our lives, so that God can look down on two single people who are purposefully dating one another, or may even be in love, and be pleased.

Chapter 2

GOD'S PROPER ORDER IN DATING

Before you hit the dating scene, I want you to be aware of God's proper order when it comes to dating, or shall I say when it comes to the pursuer and the "pursuee." I know this has been said before but it bears repeating: the man pursues the woman. I'll say it again, louder this time: the MAN pursues the WOMAN!

It is not God's will for the woman to chase after a man.

It sends the wrong signals, and it throws everything out of order. God is a God of order. *1 Corinthians 14:40* tells us, *"Let all things be done decently and in order."* God's established order for dating is found in His Word:

> *Whoso findeth a wife findeth a good thing,*
> *and obtaineth favor of the Lord.*
> *Proverbs 18:22*

This means that the *man* has been given the divine assignment and ability to find his wife! I would like to also add that the word, "findeth," in this passage of Scripture means, "to come forth, to appear, to meet or be present, to get hold upon." God brought the first man, Adam, his wife. Eve wasn't created and then started running after Adam saying, "Adam, oh Adam, here I am big boy! Don't you want to get with me?" No. God presented Eve to Adam, and Adam *recognized* her as his wife when he said, *"...This is now bone of my bones, and flesh of my flesh: she shall be called Woman, because she was taken out of Man."* (Genesis 2:23)

In today's vernacular you can say, "Man of God, God will present you with someone who may be potential wife material, but the only way you will recognize her as such is if you have a clue about

14

what you're looking for in a wife!" More than just surface stuff, a king's mother gave her son clues as to what to look for in a wife in *Proverbs 31: 10 – 31*. Man of God, you may want to allow that to be your guide instead of how fine she looks or how you can imagine getting it on with her in the bedroom.

Also note that Adam wasn't somewhere sitting on the dock of the bay telling God, "Oh, woe is me, I don't have a wife, I'm so lonely, I can't find my help meet . . . " No. It was *God's idea* to bless Adam with his help meet, not Adam's idea *(Genesis 2:18)*. Adam was already enjoying his time fellowshipping with God and allowing God to train him to be more like his Heavenly Father. God brought animals to him and allowed Adam to name them, as he was busy working for God, tilling the ground and tending to the field.

In other words, as a single, man was already operating in his purpose, walking in his calling, and working, *before* God presented the man with his wife. For the men of God reading this book, you want to already pray about and discover your purpose and walk in it, or at least take some steps toward your goals, and have a j – o – b before you go out looking for a wife! Now if you're just looking for a woman or a play thang, then that's up to you, but this book is for two people who are purposefully dating to see if the other person has the potential to become wifey.

The same thing goes for the ladies reading this book. Instead of slipping your phone number to every fine, saved brotha you meet, make sure you're taking this time, while you're *waiting to be found,* to grow in your relationship with God. Pray about and discover your purpose and actively pursue it, and continue serving God until an opportunity presents itself to pray about whether or not the man who has approached you could be the one for you.

Don't buy all this, "It's the 21st century and now women pursue men if they want to get a date," crap. I bet the person who invented this line was a man – a man who wanted to give women the green light to approach him so it can open the door for him to try and get some.

Men are hunters by nature. God designed them that way. If a man sees something he wants, he will go after it. All throughout the Bible, you see men who saw what they wanted and went after it. Take David, for example, even though he knew Bathsheba was already married to one of his faithful soldiers, when he saw her bathing on the rooftop that day, he wanted her, and he went after what he wanted! *(2 Samuel 11:2-4)* Now I'm in no way condoning adultery, but I'm just using this as an example to show that a man will go after what he wants.

Another example from the Bible is Abram's wife, Sarai. When Abram sojourned to Egypt, he told everyone Sarai was his sister, and Pharaoh wanted her and had his princes take her and present her before him in order to become his wife, until he discovered that she was already Abram's wife. *(Genesis 12:11-20)*.

Time out for all these excuses that some women make for men by proclaiming, "Oh, he's shy," or, "Oh, I just gotta help him out," No! The only time a man will need help from you is after you say, "I do" because the word, "meet" in *help meet* means to "aid." Until then, use this time to observe what this man has the ability to do on his own, and having enough courage to approach you should be one of things you observe.

So again, as mentioned earlier in this chapter, God is a God of order. Ladies, you don't have to get out of the order of God's divine assignment for the man by asking a man out on a date. A woman who asks a man out on a date is setting the foundation of the relationship. She is positioning herself in the leadership role, which belongs to the man.

For instance, if a woman asks a man out on their first date, and then they marry, then she better not be surprised when she has to take the driver's seat when the bills come due and the kids are out of control because, girlfriend, you already let that man know from jump that you were in control and that you wore the pants.

GOD'S ESTABLISHED ORDER FOR THE HOME

God's established order for the home is as such: Christ, husband, wife.

Ephesians 5:23 says, *"For the husband is the head of the wife, even as Christ is the head of the church: and he is the savior of the body."* I get it; the ladies don't want to hear this, but don't get mad at me, get mad at God because it's in the Bible! Just kidding – don't get mad at God. The reason God wrote this was to establish order.

Order is not to denote control or forced submission by the husband, but to ensure peace and harmony in the home. When you do it God's way you get God's results. So I said all this to say, ladies, when you put yourself out there and ask a man on a date, or even ask a man to marry you, you're out of order and may end up disappointed with the end result.

YOUR DUE SEASONS HAVE TO MATCH

If a man is interested, he is going to pursue you and ask you out in due season. Ladies, you have to realize that what's due season for you may not be due season for him.

A lot of men, especially Christian brothas, want to make sure they're ready mentally, spiritually, financially and physically before they start dating for the purpose of marriage. I'm not saying he has to have a million dollars in the bank, but he wants to be able to at least make sure that he can cover the cost of two people on a date! Purposefully dating someone is an investment in one's time and money, and sometimes the man just wants to make sure he's prepared.

Ladies, I'm not saying that you have to be cold or stone-faced every time you see a man of God you wouldn't mind dating, or avoid him because you don't want him to think you like him even though you really do. It's okay to smile when you meet, or speak to him in a friendly matter. Small gestures like this may let the man know that you just may be open to his advances, or at least that you won't shoot him down if he decides to ask you for your phone number. Just know that if he is interested in you, he'll pursue you. Men were born with a conquering nature.

MEN HAVE LASER BEAM FOCUS

Do you ever notice that a man who is set on a goal will stick to it no matter what? If his goal is to be married and start a family one day, and he meets you along the way and finds interest, he'll go after you. He'll inquire about you, and he'll want to get to know more about you.

Just like Boaz inquired about Ruth before he approached her, that man will do his homework about you *(Ruth 2:5-6)*. He will make sure your reputation is in line with God's Word *(Proverbs 22:1)*. There will be no room for second guessing. Which leads me to another point – ladies, if he hasn't told you, verbatim, that he's interested, then don't assume he is until he says so.

DON'T RUN WITH THE VISION!

Some men, Christian men included, like to flirt with women. I don't know if it's just to boost their ego, or if maybe they're observing you and fifty other women in the church at the same time, but some of them do flirt. Ladies, do not misread these signals as, "Oh, he likes me so he must be The One!" Instead, guard your heart like *Proverbs 4:23*, and don't allow your mind to "take you there," if he hasn't even said a word to you. Don't "run with the vision," as I often say.

In other words, if he hasn't asked you out yet, and you notice he keeps singling you out after church service, don't all of a sudden envision your wedding gown and start picking flowers for your wedding even though he hasn't even approached you. Instead, chill. Be yourself, and don't assume anything until he makes his intentions crystal clear. Besides, he may just be observing you, and he may not be ready to approach you right now – God may be working on Him about some things concerning himself right now. Whatever the case, don't go "claiming him" to your girlfriends if he hasn't even asked you for your number, or even started conversing via email or on your Facebook page.

PICK ME! PICK ME!

The one thing that Adam *didn't* have to deal with, once God presented him his mate, is the challenge that I believe every single brother has to deal with today – that's choice. Men and women of God, we *choose* who we involve ourselves with in a relationship, so don't take it personal if someone doesn't *choose you.*

If you are a person of substance who knows you will make a great husband or wife one day, chalk it up as "their loss," and keep it moving. Don't get down in the dumps, and men of God, don't take ten years to pursue the next one because you're so heartbroken that the one you wanted didn't want you in return.

Remember, God created each and every one of us with free will. Even God doesn't want us to serve Him because we feel forced to, and the same rule applies with choosing someone to date. The will is involved!

For example, Abraham charged his servant with the awesome responsibility of finding a wife for Abraham's son, Isaac. The matter was so serious that Abraham made him swear by it by putting his servant's hand underneath his thigh. I'm sure his servant was more than willing to grant Abraham's request at his dying bed, but the servant wanted to make sure that if the woman he chose for Isaac was not willing to return with him to marry Isaac, that he would not be held responsible in case she refused.

"And the servant said to him, Peradventure
the woman will not be willing to follow me unto
this land: must I needs bring thy son again
unto the land from whence thou camest?"
Genesis 24:5

Abraham replied, "And if the woman will not
be willing to follow thee, then thou shalt be clear from
this my oath: only bring not my son thither again."
Genesis 24:8

So even in biblical times the men weren't simply grabbing the women by the hair screaming, "Me, man, you, woman, you come with me, NOW!" No, clearly, in this example we can see that there is a will involved. She had to be willing to go with the servant to marry Isaac. If she was not willing, she did not have to go and Abraham's servant would have been cleared from Abraham's dying wish.

So remember, when two people decide to date and eventually marry, their will is involved. There should be no naming and claiming people! You know what I mean, ladies, you see brotha fine, new member of the church who just got saved two weeks ago and next thing you know you're claiming him to your girlfriends and asking God to give you that man to be your husband.

The same thing goes for men, I've had women tell me that men would come up to them and tell them that, "God said you were my wife," as if that's going to make her bow down to him, submit to "God's will" and marry him. What a lot of people fail to realize is that God gives us free will to choose who we end up marrying. Just like He gave us free will to decide whether or not we wanted to accept Jesus Christ as our personal Lord and Savior, we have free will to decide if we want to say, "yes," to an invitation to purposefully date or even marry someone.

If a man tells you, "God told me you were the one," ladies, you better make sure that God has told you about it, too, and that it bears in line with your spirit. Then you better pray, and still invest time in dating and getting to know one another in order to determine if he's really *it*, or a *counterfeit*!

NO NAMING AND CLAIMING PEOPLE!

Some people take *Mark 11:24* out of context which reads:

> *Therefore I say unto you, What things soever ye desire, when ye pray, believe that ye receive them, and ye shall have them.*

Some people read this and say, "Whomp! There it is! I can claim sister Shirley as my good thing because the Bible says all I have to do is believe I receive!" No, no, no, slow your roll Brotha Prayright. This Scripture says whatsoever *things* you desire, not *whosoever* you desire! It also goes on to say believe that ye receive *them*, and ye shall have *them*. Which also denotes things, and not people, because God wouldn't say you can believe you receive more than one person!

This Scripture is talking about things you're believing God for, as long as it lines up with God's will. Because people are free will agents, this Scripture does not apply to naming and claiming folks. Instead of that approach, what you can do is, when you pray for your future mate, pray that you have favor with your future mate, without attaching a name to the person. We do not have the power to control another person's free will, i.e. saying, "Lord, *make* her want me!" That's not going to happen.

Chapter 3

DATING GOD'S WAY

As mentioned in the introduction, the purpose of dating, as used in this book, is to discover, through prayer, the leading of the Holy Spirit, and through gathering information whether or not the person you are consistently and exclusively dating has the potential to be your spouse. The only way information can be gathered about the other person is to create dating environments where communication is a key component.

Date to Encourage Dialog

When I think of the word *dating* I think of the word *data*. You can look at dating as the collection of data, or information, facts, and history about another person. So many times we focus on "falling in love," with the other person while dating, instead of collecting the necessary data in order to discover whether the person we're dating is someone we should be falling in love with! This is why it's so important to date to encourage dialog.

For example, ladies, if a guy asks to take you to the movies, then after the movie he drives you home, then I would say 90% of the date consisted of staring at a big screen, which also involves almost no communication. The most communication time you may have is during the drive to and fro, which is not ample time to get to know someone, especially if it's the first date.

The first date is normally the "weeder" date where you decide whether or not the other person should be garnered a second date by the end of the date. You don't want the first date to be a time waster with barely any communication. You hardly get to know a person that way.

Now if you decide, on a first date, to do dinner and a movie, then that's different. Dinnertime is a great time to engage in dialog. Use this time to ask casual questions about one another, such as how the other person spends their free time, what he or she does for a living, and what are some of their hobbies, interests, or aspirations. You also may want to ask them how do they normally spend their weekends, which peeks into their lifestyle because if their answer is that they spend their weekends watching the game drinking beer or clubbin' then that lets you know they're not totally living for the Lord!

Ask him or her what church they attend, where they serve in their church, or how often they frequent their church. If their answer is, "I attend off and on," or, "I don't have a church home right now," or, "I don't see a real need to go to church. I read the Bible at home," (in other words, they attend Bedside Baptist every Sunday morning), use caution. If church attendance is something you value and recognize in the Word where it admonishes believers to not forsake the assembling together of other believers (Hebrews 10:25), then that may let you know that your date doesn't see the value in his own spiritual growth and development, and you may decide then and there if this is someone you would want to continue dating.

Also, as a suggestion, if he professes to be a church goer, and goes with you all the time, do what a colleague of mine did before she decided to marry her husband - she said she wasn't going to church one Sunday, and she observed to see whether or not he would still go on his own without her. Wasn't that clever? Well he did attend service without her, and let's just say now they're happily married and she's more secure in the fact that she married a true man of God and not just someone who was taking interest in her church attendance simply because he wanted to impress her or come off as someone somewhat spiritual.

Back to dialog while dating, while conversing with your date, don't use this time to talk about how your ex treated you badly, how your "baby daddy" isn't paying child support, or how you are still healing from an emotionally painful upbringing where your father left you and your mom without any explanation. Instead guard your heart, and do not let anyone into the secret place of your heart until you get to know and trust him more and develop a consistent friendship relationship first.

The Word of God says:

Keep thy heart with all diligence;
for out of it are the issues of life.
Proverbs 4:23

The word, "keep," in this passage of Scripture means to *guard, preserve,* and *maintain.* It is wise to guard, preserve, and maintain your heart when it comes to the opposite sex until you trust the other person and know that they have your best interest at heart.

You don't want to lay all your cards out on the table on the first date. This may scare your date away! Also, a nugget for the ladies, most men are problem solvers, so don't share all of your personal business and weaknesses on the first date because he may become overwhelmed with your problems which he may feel he has to solve!

Instead, just focus on getting to know each other a little better during the first date. Share your personal testimonies, and how and when you both first came to know Christ, and how your life has changed ever since. This is also a good way to tell if the other person's salvation confession is genuine.

Another idea would be to do the movie first, then dinner, because the movie could become a topic of discussion at dinnertime, which can inform you of how your date thinks and processes information.

Dating to encourage dialog is a way to get to know another person and gather more information about that other person to help determine whether or not this is someone you would like to continue dating. Have some idea about what you're looking for in a mate in advance, and discover whether or not the other person fits those qualifications by communicating.

KNOW WHAT YOU'RE LOOKING FOR BEFORE YOU DATE

For example, if, besides being saved, you value education or intelligence as an important quality you're looking for in a mate, then pay attention to how your date articulates himself. Can he form complete sentences? Does he enjoy reading? Or, if you value one with a positive outlook on life, listen to how he comments on people, places, or things during the date. Is he negative? Does he complain all the time? The more time you spend with a person and the more you pay attention to how they communicate and what they discuss, the more you gain a better indication as to how they're wired and what's really in their heart.

. . . for out of the abundance of the heart
the mouth speaketh.
Matthew 12:34

Dating to encourage dialog also decreases the chance of falling into sexual sin. There are more suggestions for date spots which encourage dialog in the Appendix section of this book. Instead of *knowing* each other with your bodies, get to know each other with your words.

BEWARE OF THE CHAMELEON

Also, beware of the, "What are you looking for in a mate?" question, because most of the time this question is asked only for the other person to hear and become what you ask for, which may not be a picture of their true selves. I call this person the "chameleon" who can change into what you ask him or her to be, simply because you told them exactly what you're looking for.

For example, if a man asks his date, "What are you looking for in a mate?" and she responds, "I'm looking for a mate who listens, and is giving, and caring, and romantic." And the next thing you know after that date she has flowers on her doorstep every week, she gets blessed with a diamond bracelet and it's not even a holiday, and every time she speaks to him he barely says two words and when she asks why he says, "I just want to listen to you and hear what you have to say." Then she may feel she struck gold and is ready to marry this man tomorrow! But then let's say she marries him . . . she shouldn't be surprised if all the lavish gifts and extra attention stops after she says, "I do," because she may discover that he was doing all those things while they were dating in order to get her to fall in love with him because she practically told him on the first date what he needed to do, verbatim, in order to win her over!

Instead of disclosing all on the first date, if asked, "what are you looking for in a mate," answer in general terms, and not specifically, so that you can *observe* how he behaves or treats you without you cluing him in on exactly what you're looking for. This way, you could observe the other person's true character instead of their ability to listen and take heed to dead giveaways. An example of a general term response could be, "I want my mate to be saved, outgoing, with a good heart." Only you know what that really means and looks like to you, and this way you're not giving it all away.

IN DATING RELATIONSHIPS, SEEK FRIENDSHIP FIRST

Two believers who decide to pursue a dating relationship together must remember that they are called to be brother and sister in Christ, first, before anything else. Before that person possibly becomes your spouse, remember that he or she is a child of God and should be treated accordingly. It is also important, in dating relationships, that the two of you seek friendship first before pursuing a romantic relationship.

Ask any married couple and they will tell you that their genuine friendship with one another is what keeps them a happily married couple – especially during those times when they get on each others' nerves. Like the old saying goes, you want to marry your best friend and true confidant. In dating relationships, you want Jesus to be the foundation used to build upon the rock of a solid friendship.

I can remember the first truly saved guy I dated at around age 21. He said he was called to the ministry, and was in the process of attending an out of state Bible college. I can remember the day before he approached me, I had just complained to God how I wanted a mate and how no one had approached me yet, and low and behold a day after I cried out to God here comes this aesthetically pleasing, nicely built brotha whom I had met at one of my church's singles ministry outings asking me if he could walk me to my car after service. Pleasantly surprised, I agreed and we exchanged numbers. From there, we talked on the phone a few times, went to a couple functions together, and next thing you know we're in a dating relationship, holding hands and being "boyfriend and girlfriend."

While he was away at Bible school, as we attempted to endure a long distance relationship, I began to realize something about him I didn't realize before. Even though we were a couple, I realized that I really didn't know him, and that I really didn't get to know him before I decided to be his girl. It was as if I just said to myself, "He's saved, I'm saved, I want a saved man of God so he must be it." Then, as we conversed even more on the phone and in person, I discovered something else about him – the fact that I didn't really like him as a boyfriend. I didn't like his dry sense of humor, and to be honest I thought he was a little boring.

I eventually broke up with him and we parted ways, but my point is before you get into a dating relationship with someone, make sure it's someone you grow to know as a friend, first, and allow the relationship to blossom from there. That way, if, along the way you determine he or she is not the one for you, then you can spare heartache and a possible lifetime of pain if you just cut it off as soon as possible. You don't want to string people along, and you don't want to waste others' time. You want to do unto others as you would have them do unto you.

Therefore all things whatsoever ye would that
men should do to you, do ye even so to them:
for this is the law and the prophets.
Matthew 7:12

DON'T RUSH THE DATING PROCESS

While the Bible denotes no set timetable as far as how long a couple should date before marriage, practical wisdom tells us that the more time you spend with someone, the more you are able to get to know the other person for who they really are. I have talked to many women who claim they didn't marry the same person they dated, but when you ask them how long they dated before marriage their normal reply is less than six months.

After dating someone for at least a year or longer you should have a more specific idea about the other person's character. True relationships, which begin with friendship as the foundation and eventually blossom into becoming each other's best friend, take time to develop. As the saying goes, "time will tell," so let time tell on a person.

You need time to get to really know each other in order to pray through the relationship, collect data, be led by the Spirit, and follow peace. You need time to see—should a situation arise where you two may not agree on something or you may be challenged—how your date responds. Does he go into a rage? Or is he calm and considers a matter before responding? Men, if peace is an important factor in choosing a wife, and she goes off on you and on other people seemingly at the drop of a hat, then you may want to ask yourself if this is the type of person you want to have to deal with for the rest of your life. During the relationship, you both want to obey the Word when it says,

Wherefore, my beloved brethren, let every man
be swift to hear, slow to speak, slow to wrath:
James 1:19

BUT MY BIOLOGICAL CLOCK IS TICKING!

As far as time goes, you don't want to just shoot for a number and say, "I want to be married by this certain age so Jerome and I need to date for about a year and then I'll expect him to give me a ring!" No, you want to let the relationship develop naturally, and not be based on your own personal timetable. Sometimes, when we do it based on our timetable, we overlook a lot of flaws about the other person that we shouldn't overlook because we feel like we're trying to get to our goal of marriage by a certain age. Don't fall into that trap. Like the song says, "Step back and let God do it."

No matter how old you are right now, no matter how much you may have thought you would have been married with 2.5 kids by now, ladies, don't get into a rush to marry the first man that comes along and says he's saved. Don't view time as an enemy. Time is your friend. If a person asks to marry you now, and you ask him to wait, then more than likely if he really loves you, he isn't going anywhere.

Invest time in your relationship in order to get to know each other better, make sure you're compatible with one another, and be 110% sure this is the person you want to spend the rest of your life with, be your spiritual head, be the father of your children (or father figure if you already have children), and spiritual covering. Deciding who you marry is the second most important decision you will make in your entire life. The most important decision was when you decided to accept Jesus Christ as your personal Lord and Savior.

DON'T MARRY JUST FOR SEX

Don't get in a rush to marry someone just because you want to have sex with them. A lot of people take this one Scripture out of context, thinking it gives Christians a license to marry the first person they want to have sex with:

> *But if they cannot contain, let them marry:*
> *for it is better to marry than to burn.*
> 1 Corinthians 7:9

In this passage of Scripture, Paul is admonishing two believers who are dating, or courting one another, to marry instead of falling into sexual sin. The point behind this Scripture is not saying marry right away, it is saying do right by God instead of sinning. It's focus is on the sin – the sin of sex outside of marriage. Instead of sinning, Paul suggests that they marry to *not* sin. However, many marry a person simply because they feel they can't control themselves. If you marry someone just because you want to have sex with them, instead of really getting to know the person and making sure you like and admire them as an individual, then you two marry, you can have sex three times a day every day, but if at the end of the day you can't stand the person you may realize that marrying simply for sex is not a good basis or foundation for a good marriage – which may cause the regular sex to eventually come to an end!

Since I believe sex is a big part of marriage for most men, some brothers make the mistake of pursuing a woman just because he can imagine enjoying having sex with her every day, all day. He may see a fine woman, with all the curves he likes, who knows how to sweet talk him and make him feel like a real man, and if on top of that he sees her in church regularly and that she has signed up to serve in an auxiliary somewhere, then she must be the one! Next thing you know he's chasing her and marrying her after a month of knowing her because he can't wait to get it on with her in the bedroom, or any other room. Then they marry, and the sex is good, but then he finds out certain things, or ways he doesn't like about her – he finds out she's selfish, that she talks down to others, hates children, and is conceited. He finds out she no longer wants to serve in the church and that she hasn't talked to her father in years. He finds out these things *after* he marries her, because he wanted her so badly that he didn't even take the necessary time to get to know her, instead he was in a rush to *know* her, know her!

Most happily married people I talk with say sex is an important piece of their relationship, but that it's not the *most* important part of their relationship. Just think about it, when two married people are 90 and 95 years old, they may not be able to perform as well as they used to in the bedroom, so what are they going to do when that happens, divorce? Or say, God forbid, if your husband has an accident and is left in a wheelchair and no longer able to perform sexually. Are you going to leave him just so you can get some on the regular again? No! Your vows should remind you, in sickness and in health, 'til death do us part, and they should cause you to stand by your husband and not allow circumstances or situations to dictate how you respond, but allow your true love and honor for that other person, and those vows made before God and man, to guide your decisions. Enjoyable companionship based on a solid friendship is the glue that helps happily married people stick together. Not just good sex.

Sexual Attraction is the Easy Part

It's easy to become sexually attracted to someone. Sexual attraction comes from the flesh, and the flesh wants what it wants, no matter if you're single, no matter if you're married and the other person is single, or no matter if you're both married to *other* people. The flesh will do every fine thing that comes its way and says the right things if it wants to! This goes for saved, sanctified, Holy Ghost-filled folks as well – the flesh does *not* discriminate! However, the key is to tame and control that savage beast known as the flesh! We will discuss five ways to tame the flesh in the next chapter. In the meantime, let's discuss some other practical ways to avoid tempting situations.

BEWARE OF DATING AT HOME!

It is possible to date someone at home. You know what I mean, the two of you are bored, so you want to just "kick it" at the other person's crib. Or maybe the brother can't afford to take you to dinner and a movie, and would rather rent a video so you two can be curled up underneath each other. Number one, if he doesn't have enough money to take you out on a date, ladies, then that may be an indication that he may not be ready to date you, because remember, the purpose of dating in *this book* is to date for the purpose of getting to know someone for the ultimate purpose to walk down the aisle. God gave the first man, Adam, an assignment, or job (*Genesis 2:15*) and this was while Adam was still single, so ladies, if that man doesn't have a job or can't afford twenty dollars to take you out, then that man is not ready to date. Besides, there are other inexpensive dating spots that won't necessarily break a brother's bank, some of which are included in my list of dating ideas found at the end of this book. But for now, let's talk about the dangers of just "chillin' at home" all the time.

LATE IN THE MIDNIGHT HOUR . . .

It is not wise to be at your date's house late at night. The later it gets, the more the temptation for "holy hands" to start to roam and become unquenchable. Why? I believe that the later it gets, the more relaxed and chilled we become, and the more our flesh gets relaxed and weak as well. I don't care how saved, sanctified, and Holy Ghost-filled you are, two saved people who are attracted to each other create a certain chemistry that oftentimes is magnified once you realize that you both are saved and your spirits are in sync. Being in someone's home or apartment late at night creates an atmosphere where the two of you can get it on where nobody has to know. The only thing is, if you slip up and have sex then the next morning both of you will know, and more importantly, God will know. And the guilt associated with sex outside of wedlock is more than even some care bear, even though we know that His mercy endures forever *(Psalm 118:1-4)*. The key is to not create the atmosphere or the opportunity for the flesh to have its way.

> *Neither give place to the devil.*
> *Ephesians 4:27*

The Amplified Bible says it this way:

> *Leave no [such] room or foothold for the devil*
> *[give no opportunity to him].*
> *Ephesians 4:27 Amp*

So do not give the devil the opportunity to have his way by allowing yourself and God's other child to get wrapped up, tied up, and tangled up in sin with each other which opens the door for the devil to have his way in your lives instead of God having His way.

In the event that you do fall into temptation, you can't say, "The devil made me do it!" No, the devil didn't make you do it! Your flesh did what it wanted to and easily succumbed to it because the stage was already set in advance. A key to preventing this from happening is to set boundaries up front.

Set Boundaries Up Front

Even before you begin dating someone, set boundaries. I recommend dating in public to avoid temptation at all costs, but if you two do end up dating at home one day, give yourselves a curfew, or a set time that the other party will have to leave. Set the curfew *before* you start dating.

Draw the line. Tell the other person that you're not going to "go there." In other words, if you have a desire to date and remain abstinent while dating (which I believe you do, otherwise you wouldn't have read this much of this book), then tell the person you're considering dating up front that you're abstinent and plan to stay that way until marriage. Most men would either stick around, or go away, and if they go away then it could mean that they weren't interested in seriously dating you in the first place. They may have just wanted to "get some" from you and once they discovered you weren't dishing out, then they'd hit the door.

Personally, because of the fact that I'm savin' it until marriage is my speaking platform and ministry, the men who approach me to date me already know up front where I stand. I've had a person I really cared about pursue me, but because he knew I wasn't about to give him any and he claimed he was so sexually needy, he eventually fell into sexual sin with someone else. Once he did that, I knew it was over for us. Sure it broke my heart, but it also let me know where he stood with God and with me. To me it's more important not to break God's heart by succumbing to having sex before marriage, instead of giving in to the sexual cravings of some man who may not have remained faithful to me or to God in the long run.

So tell the person up front. Also, ladies, beware of men who will act as if they take you at your word and respect your wishes, but then try and see how far they can go with you at every opportunity. Draw the line up front, and ladies, you take the lead in how far you will allow him to go, whether it's just holding hands, a kiss on the cheek, or resting your head on his shoulder.

THOU SHALT KNOW THYSELF

If one day, ladies, you come home from a nice afternoon date, and then you go back to his place, swing your arms around his neck and start kissing him wildly, don't be surprised when he's leading you into his bedroom. A lot of men have sex on the brain almost all the time, so your forwardness actually triggers his brain and his flesh that something's about to go down and he won't want to stop! So the best thing to do, in this case, is not start something you can't finish, especially if you've had a sexually active past. It may bring back old memories such that your body responds to the stimulus in front of it and the next thing you know your clothes are coming off. Not everyone can kiss without it leading into sex. Know your own personal struggles and convictions, and, if necessary, don't go there. And ladies, if you say you're going to be abstinent, don't take that man on a ride he can't enjoy all the way. Know that a man will go as far as you allow him to go. You're in control.

The same thing goes for men because there are some loose women out here who may want to test your loyalty to the God you serve. The Bible makes it plain as it talks about loose women who flatter with the tongue *(Proverbs 7:4-27)*. Whoever you pursue, man of God, tell that woman, up front, that you won't be having sex and carefully observe her response.

TELL THE PERSON UP FRONT THAT YOU'RE ABSTINENT BEFORE YOU DATE

Why is it so important to verbally tell the person you're considering dating up front? Because it sets the boundary, and it sets the tone of the relationship. It also reduces the chances of something "just happening" later down the line because you have verbally sealed the deal, which decreases your chances of sinning.

Words are powerful, and what you say, up front, triggers what goes into your subconscious mind which actually controls how your body responds.

For if any man offend not in word, the same is a perfect man, and able also to bridle the whole body.
James 3:2

This Scripture implies that the words we say have the ability to bridle, or control our whole bodies. In other words, your words control how your body responds!

And men of God, if that flattering woman you thought was so saved because she barely wore makeup and wore a skirt to her heels still starts coming on to you, and brushes up against you, rubbing her chest against yours, then know that she is a loose woman who is only trying to test you and your commitment to the God you serve. The Word of God cautions brothers as it says in *Proverbs 6:27*, "*Can a man take fire in his bosom, and his clothes not be burned?*"

BEWARE OF COUNTERFEITS

Realize that just like God sends us our mates to be a major blessing in our lives and help advance the kingdom of God as two put ten thousand to flight *(Deuteronomy 32:30)*, know that satan also sends counterfeits whose only plan and purpose is to get you outside of the will of God, convert you back over to *his* kingdom of wild times and loose living, and eventually take you out. So stand your ground, and always remember your commitment to God, first, as an unmarried believer. Commit to God more than you would commit to any other fallible human being who has no heaven or hell to put you in.

Chapter 4

5 Ways to Tame the Beast

Known as the Flesh

As I mentioned in Chapter 1, the flesh is a beast! Once you got saved, your spirit man received Jesus Christ as your Lord and Savior, and God came to dwell and reside in your newly created spirit. However, realize that your flesh is separate from your spirit, and the flesh wants what it wants now! The flesh wants to sin now, and repent later!

Know that man is a spirit being. We have a soul (which consists of the mind, will, and emotions), and we live in a physical body. Our mind tells our body what to do. Think about it. Every sin starts with a thought. This is another reason I say nothing, "just happens," because even before you may have missed it and slipped into sexual sin, before you "did it," more than likely you thought about that thang. You meditated on it. You may have even imagined having sex with that other person before you even had the opportunity, and saw yourself pleasing that other person and you being pleased sexually even though he or she isn't your spouse. This is why Jesus taught his disciples, *"But I say unto you, That whosoever looketh on a woman to lust after her hath committed adultery with her already in his heart." (Matthew 5:28).* So if you look on someone you're attracted to, fellas, and immediately imagine having sex with her, then you've already committed adultery in your heart. So then the "pursuit" becomes how quickly you can get her to the bedroom, instead of to the altar!

1. GUARD YOUR THOUGHT LIFE

The first way to tame the flesh is to guard your thought life. Be careful about what you think and mediate on. Men of God, if you see an attractive woman, see her as one of God's beautiful flowers, and view her as your sister, because, like I said before, we all are brothers and sisters in Christ, first, *before* we become anyone's husband or wife.

If you see a scantily clad woman leaving no room for the imagination, practice what my Bishop calls "the holy turn," which means if you happen to see her, quickly turn your head away. If you see her, immediately turn. Unfortunately, for those of you living in warmer climates, or when summertime hits you may be "holy turning" all day long, but be rest assured that God sees your heart intention. What's important is that you don't see, and keep looking, and keep looking, and then start meditating, and then next thing you know "snap!" you've taken a mental photo of that woman in your mind so now you can go home and take a nap dreaming about what you would love to do with that woman you saw earlier that day. That's what you *don't* want to do.

And ladies, help the brothers out. Especially in the church. Most of us know men are visual beings, so don't wear clothes where your girls are hanging all out or your pants or skirt is so tight you can barely breathe! Let's not become stumbling blocks for our brothers in the Lord. If you don't want to be viewed as a sex object, then don't wear clothes that make you look like one. Besides, if God has blessed you with a nice figure, trust me, that man is going to notice you whether you have on a tight mini-skirt or a loose skirt hanging all the way to the floor. So don't try and entice a man by the clothes you wear. Keep a nice balance and know that it is possible to dress stylish and not provocatively, while still feeling good about what you're wearing. Be mindful of the "message" that your outfit is sending the people you come in contact with on a daily basis. Take inventory of your wardrobe. Do some spring cleaning if necessary. The next time you get dressed, ask *God*, "How do I look?" and see what *He* says, especially before you go out on a date.

Enough of that side journey (that was free, by the way :0), another way to guard your thought life is to spend a lot of your time serving and pleasing God.

Commit thy works unto the Lord, and thy
thoughts shall be established.
Proverbs 16:3

So does this mean that working unto the Lord and serving Him helps establish your thoughts? Yes! The word, "establish," means to call attention or admonition. So as you work for God and serve Him then He calls attention and admonishes your thought life. And what does God want you to think on?

". . . whatsoever things are true, whatsoever things are honest, whatsoever things are just, whatsoever things are pure, whatsoever things are lovely, whatsoever things are of good report; if there be any virtue, and if there be any praise, think on these things."
Philippians 4:8

Serving God, as a single believer, helps establish your thought life, and helps you think on things God would have you think on. Besides, as single saints, we should be about our Father's business now, serving in our local church and being a blessing to all those we encounter.

*But I would have you without carefulness. He that
is unmarried careth for the things that belong to the
Lord, how he may please the Lord: But he that is
married careth for the things that are of the world,
how he may please his wife.*
1 Corinthians 7:32-33

As an unmarried believer, your main focus should be to please God, and to care about the things that belong to the Lord. Once you get married, your focus shifts from pleasing God to pleasing your spouse, because in pleasing your spouse God will be pleased. Marriage should be an outpouring of the lifelong love affair that you already established first, with God, as a single believer.

Practice oneness with God now, and use this time to grow in your relationship with Him, and allow all other decisions made in your life to be based on whether or not that particular decision will please God. A decision to remain abstinent until marriage pleases God. A decision to read this book in order to learn how to be kept by God, pleases God. As long as God is pleased and remains number one in your life, He'll make sure that He continues to bless and please you.

CONTINUE IN GOD'S WORD DAILY

A final way to guard your thought life is to read God's Word daily. As you read God's Word, His Word gets ingrained in your spirit and the more you feed your spirit, the more you starve the flesh. The flesh is in a constant battle every day. It's not just a one time thing – you don't just get saved one day and then, "poof!" all of your desires for sex are gone. No, sanctification, or the practice of being set apart from the world and the world's way of doing things, is a daily process. The flesh has to die daily. Even Paul says in *1 Corinthians 15:31* *". . . I die daily."* meaning he dies to himself and his own fleshly desires daily. Paul also says in *Galatians 5:24* *"And they that are Christ's have crucified the flesh with the affections and lusts."* The best way to crucify the flesh, or extinguish or subdue passion or selfishness, which is what the word *crucify* means, is to feed your spirit man with the Word of God.

The Word of God is the will of God and the power of God.

When you read the Word, God's power gets implanted in your spirit man, affects your thoughts, and it comes with an anointing that will cause you to be kept by God.

Now unto him that is able to keep you from falling,
and to present you faultless before the presence
of his glory with exceeding joy.
Jude 1:24

God wants to present you faultless to the presence of His glory, and He's the one that's going to continue to keep you, as you remain in His presence and consistently remain in His Word.

For the Word of God is quick, and powerful,
and sharper than any twoedged sword, piercing
even to the dividing asunder of soul and spirit,
and of the joints and marrow,
an is a discerner of the
thoughts and intents of the heart.
Hebrews 4:12

God's Word is the keeping power, and it also discerns the thoughts and intentions of the heart. The more Word you get in you, the more His desires become your desires, and His thoughts become your thoughts.

Consider yourself a garden - the more seed of the Word you sow into yourself as you read it and meditate on it each day, even if it's just a Scripture or two, the more you have the potential to grow up and become that strong, deeply rooted and grounded, settled and prosperous tree planted by the rivers of water as described in *Psalm 1:3*.

As you read God's Word daily, meaning more than just on Sunday as you follow along with the pastor, you will notice that you will begin thinking differently about a lot of things. Your mind will start conforming to God's mind.

For example, I mentioned in Chapter 1 of this book that even though I got saved, I didn't stop clubbin' until a year later. Well, I can remember one night when the black caucus at my college dorm had a club-like party in the cafeteria. I attended with some friends, and this was soon after I had attended my current church and was getting a little more involved in the things of God. Well, I went upstairs to go to the gig, but as I entered the dark room and looked around and noticed all the sexually suggestive type dancing that was going on around me, and then I really starting listening to the words of the music that was being played, I suddenly felt out of place. Even though I was the same girl who, just the other week, was going to almost every campus party and chanting the words to almost every degrading "booty" song right along with the rest of my all girl crew.

For some reason, tonight was different. That reason, I believe, was because God's Word started to take root on the inside of me, which got a hold of my mind as I thought to myself, "What the heck am I doing here? I need to get outta here, I *don't* belong." So I left. I left the club life behind and decided to pursue God's perfect will for my life.

You see, God doesn't want you to just get saved and that's it. *Romans 12:1-2* says,

> *"I beseech you therefore brethren, by the*
> *mercies of God, that ye present your bodies a living*
> *sacrifice, holy, acceptable unto God, which is your*
> *reasonable service. And be not conformed to this world:*
> *but be ye transformed by the renewing of your mind,*
> *that ye may prove what is that good, and acceptable,*
> *and perfect will of God."*

Presenting our bodies as a living sacrifice to God is our reasonable service, or the least that we can do seeing as though He has done so much for us. Once we get saved we are not to conform to the world but we are to be transformed by the renewing of our mind.

The word "renew" means, renovation.

God wants our minds to become renovated with His way of thinking.

Think of an old, dilapidated eye sore of a home that needs to be renovated. It may be in desperate need of a paint job, have burst pipes, and it may be abandoned with weeds growing around it and all over the place. If anyone were to even consider purchasing that home it would possibly require thousands of dollars worth of renovation.

Now think about before you were saved.

Before you were saved you were like that home in need of serious repair. You were dead to Christ, your thought life was in the toilet, and your mind was dark. You were blinded to the truth. But once you got saved, glory to God, your eyes were opened and now you see! Now you see that Jesus is your Lord, now you see that you need God in your life and without Him you are nothing! Now you see that death does not belong to a believer, because once he makes his transition from this earth he goes home to forever be with the Lord in his very own mansion in heaven!

However, you received a supernatural renovation, but that's not all that needs renovating.

Your mind also needs to be renovated, or renewed. As you continue in God's Word, the light bulb will come on even brighter as you receive further renovation in your mind. Now you see that God's only desire is to bless and prosper you *(Psalm 35:27)*, now you see that God has a divine plan for your life and that He only desires to give you peace and not evil *(Jeremiah 29:11)*, now you see God's way of doing things, including the truth that not engaging in sex before marriage is not God's way of robbing you of any fun or "hating on you," but that it is so that He can purge you from your old ways, preserve you, protect you, and prepare you for the life that He has for you - a life far better than you could ever dream, hope for, or imagine!

> *But the path of the just is as the shining light, that*
> *shineth more and more unto the perfect day.*
> *Proverbs 4:18*

So continue in God's Word daily to have your mind constantly renewed and renovated to God's way of thinking, and He will continue to order your steps as you keep conforming your will to His will and obeying His commands.

2. GUARD THE GATES!

A second way to tame the flesh is to "guard the gates," more specifically the eye and ear gates.

Job 31:1 says, "I made a covenant with mine eyes; why then should I think upon a maid?"

The Amplified Bible makes it plain as *Job 31:1* reads, *"I dictated a covenant (an agreement) to my eyes; how then could I look [lustfully] upon a girl?"*

In this passage of Scripture, Job, a man of God indeed, is demonstrating how he made a personal covenant, or commitment to God, Himself, to not even look lustfully at a woman. Job is demonstrating how he is guarding, or protecting his eyes from even "going there."

In today's society, especially with images of sex being advertised on seemingly every billboard and every television commercial, you have to make a special effort to be careful about what you set your eyes upon, so you don't look lustfully after it and arouse the flesh.

This is another reason why it is so important for believers not to get caught in satan's trap of viewing pornography, whether in a magazine, on a video, or online. The greek word, "porneia," means harlotry, idolatry, and fornication. As you look lustfully on these images, the spirit upon it, which is definitely *not* the Holy Spirit, defiles your own spirit. It causes you to view the opposite sex as merely a sex object, even during day to day encounters with people in general, you begin to undress people with your eyes.

I have heard of marriages which were shattered and almost broken because their spouses were addicted to letting their eye gates get a hold of this filth and allowing the enemy to have his way, subtly, tricking the person viewing it into thinking he's not doing anything wrong since he or she isn't actually having sex, but simply viewing it. However, viewing it is not protecting your eye gates.

I will set no wicked thing before mine eyes: I hate the work of them that turn aside; it shall not cleave to me.
Psalm 101:3

Setting no wicked thing before your eyes includes not allowing your eyes to watch porn, or even certain 'R' rated movies you know you shouldn't watch because you know by watching it alone will make you want to go out and get some, and as single Christians we don't have that option.

I'm led to continue with the online piece. You also want to be careful about subtle traps the enemy may set online which may not be as obvious as a porn site, but beware of cruising certain social networking sites such as MySpace or Black Planet where a lot of folks on there are scantily clad or even in just their underwear! Don't get caught up in that trap either; shut the computer off, if necessary, or even block yourself from being able to view certain websites or images. Protect your eye gates, so it doesn't seep into your spirit man and defile your heart and the anointing of God on your life.

The Apostle Paul says *1 Corinthians 9:27*, *"But I keep under my body, and bring it into subjection: lest that by any means, when I have preached to others, I myself should be a castaway."* The Amplified Bible version of *1 Corinthians 9:27* reads, *"But [like a boxer] I buffet my body [handle it roughly, discipline it by hardships] and subdue it, for fear that after proclaiming to others the Gospel and things pertaining to it, I myself should become unfit [not stand the test, be unapproved and rejected as a counterfeit]."*

Paul makes a bold proclamation as he describes how he handles his own body roughly and disciplines it by hardships so that he won't become unfit in the pulpit, or be regarded as a hypocrite – preaching one thing and living another. So Paul obviously lets us know that keeping the flesh under subjection and under obedience to the will of God is no easy task, so much so that he handles it roughly. So when it comes to your eye gates, start by making a covenant with God and your eyes to not look lustfully on someone else; do the "holy turn" as often as necessary, and handle your body roughly by bringing it under subjection to God's Word and God's will.

WHO'S GOT YOUR EAR?

You also want to guard your ear gates. Have you ever noticed how if you hear a certain song over and over, then all of a sudden, when you're not listening to any music at all, you find yourself singing that very song or hearing its melody being replayed in your mind? That's because what you were hearing over and over again, also known as a form of meditation, was getting inside your ear gates and again, seeping into your heart, so much so that you started singing what you had been hearing. The Word tells us in *Ephesians 5:19, "Speaking to yourselves in psalms and hymns and spiritual songs, singing and making melody in your heart to the Lord."* It's fine for us to meditate on and speak to ourselves in songs and sing songs, as long as they're unto the Lord.

A lot of the stuff on the radio that gets played regularly on the secular stations are not songs that glorify God, but glorify premarital sex, adultery, and fornication. I'm not saying it's a sin to listen to a secular station, but I am cautioning you to guard your ear gates, and what you allow yourself to hear consistently gets into your mind and eventually comes out of your mouth. Instead of listening to songs that preach that "there ain't nothing wrong with a little bump and grind," you may want to listen to songs that uplift, encourage, and inspire, such as gospel music and songs meant to motivate you.

GOSPEL MUSIC CAN KEEP YOU

What we hear also affects how we respond in certain tempting situations. I can remember a time as a young teenager when I had a boy over and we were in the basement listening to the radio. We were both standing, and he decided to head towards me and give me a hug and more than likely a kiss, but all of a sudden the weirdest thing happened – suddenly, a gospel song came on this particular secular radio station. I believe it was a BeBe and CeCe Winans song, but I'm not sure. Let's just say as soon as that song came on, this young man took his hands off of me and we just stood there looking at each other.

He and I both knew that what we were hearing glorified God and not what we were about to do, so I guess it was another way God was keeping me from this tempting situation. So allow what you listen to on a regular basis to keep you as well.

If you ever feel horny, or have the urge to want to go out and get some, or maybe the temperature may be rising on the inside and you're in the car about to go over to Lajaneequa's house who you know is ready to dish it out at any given moment, play a Donnie McClurkin song or any other gospel music, and I'm sure, soon enough, that urge will go away. Listen to praise and worship the next time, single believer, you get the urge to have sex. The flesh may not want to hear it at the time, but your spirit man will be thankful you did.

Finally brethren, whatsoever things are true, whatsoever things are honest, whatsoever things are just, whatsoever things are pure, whatsoever things are lovely, whatsoever things are of good report; if there be any virtue, and if there be any praise, think on these things.
Philippians 4:8

So as I mentioned previously, what you hear over and over affects what you think and meditate on, and, again, every sin starts with a thought.

If you constantly listen to songs that talk about, "ready to go right now," with an, "LOL smiley face," then the words of those songs get ingrained in your mind and if the next thing you know you're calling your ex asking to meet him or her at your place. And when ya'll have sex and you wake up the next morning feeling all guilty and confused, don't "blame it on the alcohol." It's because of what you've been meditating on, in the form of what you've been allowing in your ear gates to become your chief motivator. This gave you the desire to call that person up and take care of what you wanted to take care of because you did not guard your ear gates.

WHO IS YOUR CREW?

Guarding your ear gates also involves who you allow yourself to hang around and listen to. It is a good idea to have close friends you fellowship with on a regular basis who believe like you believe as it pertains to premarital sex. As you and I both know, not everyone who claims to be saved has adopted all of God's expectations as their own, including not having sex until marriage. If most of your friends sit up and have long conversations about sex, and how good it was for them last night, or how this weekend your good girlfriend plans on calling her ex because even though he got on her nerves, he still made her feel good in bed, then at the end she says, "I'll repent afterwards," and everyone laughs, then you shouldn't be hanging around those type of people. Why? Because as they're speaking their words are infiltrating your ear gates, and their words are influencing you, whether you realize it or not.

Premarital sex as a single believer is not something that should be taken lightly or joked about. Some people make excuse for their promiscuous lifestyle by proclaiming, "God know my heart! If I ask for forgiveness, God'll forgive me." And they treat allowing men to go up inside them just like it's any other sin such as lying or swearing. I do believe that there is no such thing as a big sin, or small sin; in God's eyes all sin is sin and it is all unpleasing to Him, but God, Himself, makes a distinction between the sin of sex outside of marriage versus any other sin.

Flee fornication. Every sin that a man doeth is without the body; but he that committeth fornication sinneth against his own body. What? Know ye not that your body is the temple of the Holy Ghost which is in you, which ye have of God, and ye are not your own?
1 Corinthians 6:18-19

In other words, Paul is saying here that every sin, *every* sin man could possibly commit is done *without* the body, except for the sin of fornication. When you fornicate, your body is taking in another person's body and defiling the temple where God lives. God made a proclamation in the New Testament that no longer will He dwell in tabernacles made by man's hands, but that He will now live and reside in man's born again body, or temple.

. . . ye are the temple of the living God; as God hath
said, I will dwell in them, and walk in them; and I will
be their God, and they shall be my people.
2 Corinthians 6:16

God loves us so much, that no longer do we have to go to a priest to hear Him speak to us like they had to do in the Old Testament; God wanted His Spirit to live inside of us to teach, comfort, and direct. He chose to live in us, so He can be closer to us, so we can have access to His power and grace, so He can speak through us, so He can use us, and so we can be endued with power from on high to be able to live right, talk right, pray right, and stay right *(Jude 1:24)*.

So if God loves us that much where He is living in us, how do you think God feels when we allow an unclean thing to come inside of us and invade the very home or dwelling place where He lives – in our bodies? Not to say the other *person* is unclean, but the *act* of ignoring God's commandment by having sex outside of the marital covenant is unclean to God. It defiles the very place where God lives. That's why, if you have sex as a single believer and then wake up feeling guilty it's because you have just defiled the very place where God lives.

The word, "defile," in Webster's 1828 dictionary means, *to make unclean, to render foul or dirty, to make impure, to tarnish, and to pollute.* The reason you may feel dirty the morning after is because of the God consciousness within you that lets you know that what just took place the night before was wrong in the sight of your Creator. Actually, you *want* to feel bad if you just missed God and had sex outside of marriage, because it lets you know that you have an awareness of the presence of God, and more than likely when you repent you'll be sincere in your heart with the intention of never committing that sin again. It's when you consistently follow a promiscuous lifestyle, forgetting to repent and not even feeling bad at all about what you just did that you should be worried, because then you have just let your own ego take control, and e.g.o., according to author, Ed Gray, stands for "Edging God Out."

So you may fool the folks at your church home if you continue in an unrepentant, promiscuous lifestyle, but know that you're definitely not fooling God, who sees all and knows all, and more importantly, He knows where your heart is and whether or not you are receptive about governing your life according to His precepts and commandments, and not your own. Because when you live according to your own laws and commands, and ignore the part where God says, "Flee fornication," then you will get your own results, or even worse, you allow satan to have access and wreak havok in your life because you chose to live according to his laws and commands, and not God's. However, be of good cheer, because if you do it God's way, you'll get God's results, and you'll walk in the favor of God and the blessings of God, and you'll go from glory, to glory, to glory in your life.

3. DON'T BE GUILTY BY ASSOCIATION

So I said all this to say, make it a priority to become close friends with other believers who are abstinent like you are. All of my really good, single friends are either abstinent or virgins. We share the same views about sex before marriage that God shares, which is that sex is a beautiful thing to be preserved for your spouse. It's not like I made sure they were all abstinent before we became close friends either – for the most part, you attract who you are even in friendship relationships, and your beliefs, convictions, and lifestyle is a magnet which draws other people like you to you.

The Word of God talks about iron sharpening iron (*Proverbs 17:17*), so a third way to tame the flesh is to make sure you have close friends who share your same belief in this area, so that if you grow weak in the flesh you can honestly go to one of them about your feelings and you can sharpen one another so that where one is weak, the other can make you strong.

Some of you reading this may think it is mean or "un-Christianlike" to not accept everyone as your close friend, including unbelievers or believers whose mind has yet to be renewed in this area, but please hear my heart on this, when I say close friend, I am speaking of the person you truly confide in, who you're running this race called life together with, and who you depend on for encouragement and motivation. Some may argue that even Jesus ate with sinners. But know that His purpose for dining with them was to be a Light and to share the gospel, not so they can chat about what went down last night with His boys and some girl down the street.

As the scribes and Pharisees questioned why Jesus ate with the sinners and publicans, Jesus' response was, ". . . *They that are whole need not a physician but they that are sick. I came not to call the righteous, but sinners to repentance."* (Luke 5:31-32) Also know that Jesus' truly close friends, or crew, were a group of twelve men who shared His vision for winning souls and shared His love for God. They were the ones whom Jesus taught and shared His most intimate secrets and stories with. And only three of them - Peter, James, and John - were the ones He confided in and asked to pray for Him the night before He was crucified when He said, ". . . *My soul is exceeding sorrowful unto death*. . . " (Mark 14:34)

We are to all work out our own salvation with fear and trembling, and while we do not have the opportunity to choose who we're related to, we can definitely choose who we let into our close circle of friends. We love everyone, but we *choose* who we call our best and closest friends.

I am a companion of all them that fear thee, and of
them that keep thy precepts.
Psalm 119:63

But now have I written unto you not to keep company,
if any man that is called a brother be a fornicator, or
covetous, or an idolator, or a railer, or a drunkard, or an
extortioner; with such a one no not to eat.
1 Corinthians 5:11

Let no man deceive you with vain words: for
because of these things cometh the wrath of God
upon the children of disobedience.
Be not ye therefore partakers with them.
For ye were sometimes darkness, but now are ye
light in the Lord: walk as children of the light.
(For the fruit of the Spirit is in all goodness and

righteousness and truth;)
Proving what is acceptable unto the Lord.
And have no fellowship with the unfruitful works
of darkness, but rather reprove them.
Ephesians 5:6-11

4. Walk in the Spirit

A fourth way to tame the beast known as the flesh is to walk in the Spirit. The more you walk in the Spirit, as opposed to walking in the flesh, the more you will not give in to temptations brought to the flesh. A lot of us are familiar with the Scripture, *"...the spirit indeed is willing, but the flesh is weak."* *(Matthew 26:41)* and some of us use that Scripture as a basis to justify what's about to go down later on tonight in the form of sexual sin. However, once you look at the context of this particular Scripture that Jesus said, you will notice that He said it the night before he was about to be crucified.

He told this to his three closest friends and disciples, Peter, James, and John, right after He got through praying for at least an hour about what was going to happen to Him the next morning on the cross. Before Jesus went into His own private prayer session in the Garden of Gethsemane, He, Himself, was weak in the flesh and didn't want, or feel like doing God's will as He proclaimed, *". . . O my Father, if it be possible, let this cup pass from me . . ."* (Matthew 26:42)

Jesus was crying out to God asking for another way to fulfill the mission of saving the world from their sins; He didn't want to have to go through the pain associated being nailed to a cross, pierced in his sides, and suffering a severe lashing that was so harsh that by the time they were done with Him He didn't even resemble a man *(Isaiah 52:14)*. But Jesus realized the ultimate purpose for His sacrifice, so instead of giving up, or giving in to the flesh, Jesus decided to go pray, and by the time He came out of the garden He changed His tune and said, *". . . nevertheless not as I will, but as thou wilt."* (Matthew 26:39).

So, just like Jesus, the first thing you want to do in order to walk in the Spirit is pray.

Prayer is simply communication with God. You can pray, everyday, in the morning to help start you on your way *(Psalm 63:1)*. Another good reason to pray first thing in the morning is because God may have specific instructions for you to fulfill within that particular day, or He may even want to warn you of something yet to come *(John 16:13)*. He may bring a Scripture to your mind and before the day is over you may have an opportunity to put that very same Scripture to the test.

Praying first thing in the morning also puts you in a spiritual mindset which lasts throughout the entire day; and it causes you to respond more positively to daily challenges, or be able to deal with difficult people who may try and test your faith. It'll cause you to walk in love throughout the day and "stay saved." I know for me, personally, if I let a few days go by without getting in morning prayer time with God, the smallest little thing would get on my nerves, but when I'm in consistent, daily communion with the Father, then my day goes a lot smoother and I operate in more of an attitude of gratitude.

THE BATTLE – IT'S *On!*

We must realize that there is a daily battle going on. Just like with any war having two sides, the battle going on with believers is the battle between the flesh and the Spirit.

For the flesh lusteth against the Spirit, and the Spirit against the flesh: and these are contrary the one to the other: so that ye cannot do the things that ye would.
Galatians 5:17

The flesh wants its way, while the real you – the God in you, wants its way. This Scripture even goes on to say how the flesh will have you doing things you, yourself, wouldn't even normally do. Man of God, you know it's not like you to look lustfully on a woman, then go home dreaming about her. Woman of God, you know it's not like you to feel so lonely that you decide to call your ex just because you feel like going out and want a man to compliment you on how beautiful you look in your new outfit, then later ask you to come inside his place afterwards and you willfully go knowing that it's getting late. Paul put it this way when he said, *"For I know that in me (that is, in my flesh) dwelleth no good thing: for to will is present with me; but how to perform that which is good I find not. For the good that I would I do not: but the evil which I would not, that I do."* (Romans 7:18-19)

So even Paul, clearly a man of God inspired by the Holy Ghost to pen two-thirds of the Bible, honestly admits to having a flesh problem. Like I said before, the flesh is a beast!

But Paul's solution, and God's solution is to walk in the Spirit daily, so not to walk in the flesh which only leads to destruction and possibly death.

For he that soweth to his flesh shall of the flesh
reap corruption; but he that soweth to the Spirit
shall of the Spirit reap life everlasting.
Galatians 6:8

The word, "corruption," means *destroy or perish.* So if you, as a believer, continue to sow to your flesh by allowing it to have its way and do what it wants to do all the time, then eventually you will reap corruption or destruction. The law of seed, time, and harvest is always at work, even when it comes to our bodies and the flesh *(Genesis 8:22).* However, when you sow to the Spirit you will reap life everlasting, or a life spent eternally in heaven with God the Father.

HOW TO WALK IN THE SPIRIT

So the question remains how do you walk in the Spirit? One of the ways we discussed is through prayer. The more you pray, the more you sow to your Spirit and actually kill the flesh. The more you run to God about situations and issues which may arise in your dating relationship, the more God will be willing and ready to hear your words, and then speak to you and minister to your spirit man as far as what you should do or how you should respond (remember, prayer is two-way communication – you speaking to God and Him speaking back to you. You know it's God's voice when His response lines up with His Word, which means the more Word you have in you, the more He can bring His Word back to your remembrance concerning your situation). However, a lot of times aside from us asking God to tell us, "if this is the one," we leave God out of the entire dating process and don't even pray to Him concerning our prospective mate. Instead of trusting our own intuition while dating, we should invite God on the date with us, and ask Him how *He* thinks it went when we return home.

Another way we walk in the Spirit is when we read God's Word daily. If not an entire chapter a day, sometimes you can study and meditate on one verse and that verse can carry you throughout the entire day. Just like most of us require three meals a day in order to feed our bodies, our spirit requires at least one meal from God's Word a day in order to feed our spirits. Besides, your spirit man is the *real you* – we just happen to have a soul and live in a body, but sometimes folks care more about their physical bodies than about feeding their own spirit man. By feasting on only one spiritual meal a week on Sunday, our spirit man goes malnourished then we wonder why we weren't able to resist temptation and fell into sexual sin when we were starving our spirit and feeding our flesh, instead of the other way around!

Think about it.

Your flesh is being fed something every single day. Every single day! Whether it's walking down the street and you notice advertisements with scantily clad women, department stores playing raunchy music, TV shows showing you two women kissing each other, movies with sex scenes, co-workers who refuse to adhere to dress codes, and the list goes on and on. So if you decide to open your Bible just once a week, or feed your spirit man once a week, while every day your flesh is fed each day all day, no wonder that beast within could just rise up at any moment and lash out!

We should strive to go to church more than just once a week, and we should definitely crack open the Bible at least once a day. As we read, and it is also a good idea to read Scripture out loud if possible, then we must also believe in the power of God that seeps through the pages.

*For the word of God is quick, and powerful, and
sharper than any two-edged sword, piercing even to the
dividing asunder of soul and spirit, and of the joints
and marrow, and is a discerner of the thoughts
and intents of the heart.*
Hebrews 4:12

We must believe that God's Word is God, Himself,
manifested in Word form.

*In the beginning was the Word, and the Word
was with God, and the Word was God.*
John 1:1

We must believe that His Word is the keeping
power of God.

*Now unto him that is able to keep you from falling,
and to present you faultless before the presence of his
glory with exceeding joy,*
Jude 1:24

I know for me, personally, it is only through the
grace of God and the Word of God that He has kept
me from having sex before marriage. It wasn't my
own doing, because if it were up to me I would have
had sex a long time ago! I had my first "boyfriend"

in kindergarten and my first french kiss before third grade. I didn't get saved until age 19 and just before attending college I was "mad" because I hadn't had sex yet. But now that I am saved and on fire for God, I thank God for His grace, mercy, and keeping power manifested in my life. It's also because of God's Word consistently sown in my heart each day that provides the necessary power in order to sustain.

Just think of the times when you were weak in the flesh. Ladies, think of when you were most vulnerable, or most sad about being single, whether it was Valentine's Day, or another Christmas rolling around with no permanent boo to hold on to, or whether it was just spring fever or you just got tired of seeing folks walking around malls all hugged up and there you were still single with no one to call your own. I can feel your pain, because I have shared it. However, when I think back on the times when I felt that way in the past, it was times when I was not spending consistent fellowship time in prayer with God, the Father, and when I wasn't reading His Word on a consistent, daily basis like I should have been. The Word of God says, *"...The joy of the Lord is your strength." (Nehemiah 8:10)*, and when I make it an on-purpose habit to set aside some time first thing in the morning for just me and Daddy, then I can honestly say that I am truly content, and that the joy of the Lord *is* my strength. Hallelujah!

God doesn't want us to just read His Word for the sake of doing our "spiritual duty" for the day. No. He wants us to grow up in the Word.

> *As newborn babes, desire the sincere milk*
> *of the word, that ye may grow thereby:*
> 1 Peter 2:2

The more Word we get sown in our hearts, the more we become the perfected, or matured saints whose mind is now confirmed to God's Word, God's will, and God's ways. If you just got saved recently, rather than think about dating, your main focus should be growing in God's Word and His ways and having a conformed mind to His will.

Once you do this by spending time in God's Word, serving in church, and attending service whenever the doors are open, then you will develop a love for God and a mind that will help control your behavior when placed in dating situations. You won't want to have pre-marital sex, because your mind has been renewed in that area and no matter what society says, or what your momma 'nem say, or even your friends say, you are not going to compromise your beliefs for the sake of thirty minutes or one night which may cost you your life or your fellowship with God.

85

You want to be able to freely go to God in prayer, and in worship, lifting up holy hands without wrath or doubting, and not feel guilty about what went on the night before.

I will therefore that men pray every where, lifting up
holy hands, without wrath and doubting.
1 Timothy 2:4

I beseech you therefore, brethren, by the mercies of
God, that ye present your bodies a living sacrifice, holy,
acceptable unto God, which is your reasonable service.
Romans 12:1

Again, Jesus paid the ultimate sacrifice on the cross when He died for our sins, the least we can do is crucify our flesh by offering our bodies unto God as a sacrifice until we get married. Paul even goes on to mention that as a Christian, being abstinent until marriage should actually be a given.

But fornication, and all uncleanness, or covetousness,
let it not be once named among you, as becometh saints.
Ephesians 5:3

Paul is saying fornication should not even be named among us as saints, or believers. I missed the memo that came out which said it is now "okay" for Christians to have pre-marital sex. Last time I checked Jesus was the same yesterday, today, and forever. I don't care how many of your current friends are so-called enjoying a lifestyle of out-of-wedlock sex, as Christians we are called to go against the grain.

We are not to conform to this world.

Even if it seems like we're the only ones on this earth who are single and not having sex before marriage, God will see you amongst millions and say to you, "Well done, thou good and faithful servant." Isn't He the one we're supposed to be living to please anyway?

HOW TO DEAL WITH A LUST PROBLEM

If you can't stop thinking and talking about sex, or if every person you find attractive you automatically undress with your eyes, but you're saved and love God, then you may be dealing with a lust problem.

A lust problem arises when we focus too much of our energy on this natural world and not spend enough time in prayer to God and in consecration through His Word. As I mentioned previously, the flesh is automatically fed every day because of the visually stimulating, sex-driven society that we live in now. It is up to us to crucify the flesh by feeding

87

our spirit man. The Word of God says we are to work out our own salvation with fear and trembling *(Philippians 2:12)*.

Just because you get saved doesn't mean you automatically become this spiritual giant who grows spiritually on a Scripture or two every other Sunday. No, you must crucify the flesh and keep it under subjection – daily. As I mentioned before, even the Apostle Paul, who lived his entire life as a single eunuch by choice, dedicating his entire life to singleness so he could serve God exclusively, admitted to having a flesh problem.

Paul crucified his flesh every single day. In *1 Corinthians 15:31* he says, *". . . I die daily."* Here he's not speaking of physical death, he's talking about dying to himself and to his flesh daily. You have to die to yourself each day. You have to get to a point where you just don't trust yourself – or shall I say your flesh.

Which leads me to another point. During the process of dying to yourself daily, crucifying the flesh, reading the Word each day and praying and praising God at church among the saints and at home, know that God sees your commitment and is pleased, and will reward you *(Hebrews 11:6)* but also know that satan sees what you are doing and is extremely angry.

Remember, satan wants to trip you up and eventually steal, kill, and destroy you *(John 10:10)*. He wants to steal your joy, your finances, your home, your family, and your destiny. He hates you, and he wants you dead.

SATAN KNOWS YOUR WEAKNESS

For instance, you may be praying in the Spirit and going weeks without falling into sexual sin, but then the next thing you know, seemingly out of the blue, here comes this fine sister with everything you like and all the right curves just how you like them asking for your phone number. Know that satan knows your weakness, ladies and gentleman, and even during periods of sincere consecration he will send exactly what you like right in front of your face in order to tempt you.

Remember, satan tempted Jesus in the wilderness after Jesus had fasted 40 days. What's the first thing a man wants after having not eaten 40 days straight – food! So the next thing you know Jesus is in the wilderness with satan and the first thing satan tries to tempt Jesus with is challenging Him to turn stones into bread so He could eat *(Matthew 4:2-3)*.

In the same manner, you may have gone 40 days without sex, you may have read this book and said you were going to read at least a Scripture a day and pray for at least 30 minutes each morning, but on that 41st day here comes that old boyfriend calling, asking if he can come over. Know that at your weakest point, satan may send you something that may look good to the eye, but is totally bad for you.

For every temptation sent your way, know that God will always create a way of escape for you (1 Corinthians 10:13).

Don't even allow the enemy to open any doors in your life.

Close any and all doors immediately.

Do not call that ex back and definitely do not stop by and visit, I don't care how much you try and convince yourself that you just want to go over there and have Bible study. Again, don't trust yourself.

THEY DON'T HAVE A CLUE

It's just like a man who was an alcoholic and just successfully completed AA's 12-step program and has been clean for three months now. If his buddies ask him to go out to the bar one night, it would be best for him to say, "No, thanks" because he may be tempted by his environment and the smell of the alcohol around him and may end up right back in the same bondage he was delivered from simply because he accepted an invitation. To his friends he may have seemed rude to say no, but his so-called friends may not have a clue about what he's been going through. They may not have a clue about the hell on earth he has gone through, and the toll his addiction has taken on himself and his family. They may not have a clue, but he definitely remembers, and he is determined to steer clear from that addiction and continue to walk in his newfound freedom from bondage.

In the same regard, folks may not have a clue about your own sexual struggles. If you've had a promiscuous lifestyle in the past and know you love sex and used to not be able to get enough of it, it may be a good idea that you not go over the house or apartment of the person you're dating alone - instead date in public places, date with other couples, and date on the phone.

5. Practice Daily Sanctification

A fifth and final way to tame the flesh is to practice daily sanctification.

As believers, we must be sanctified.

The Word "sanctify" in Webster's dictionary means, *"to separate or set apart."* Once we accept God's call into the army of the living God, we are to answer to our Commander in Chief, God, and be set apart, or separate from the world. Sure, we are *in* the world, but we are not to be *of* the world. The world, nor what all of our friends are doing, nor what our parents say, nor what the media or Hollywood says, should not govern how we act or think. How we act or think should be controlled by the Word of God, with the B-I-B-L-E as life's instruction manual.

Sanctification is not a dress code. Just because Sister Show 'Nuff Pray Right comes to church every week with a loose skirt down to her ankles and no makeup on doesn't mean she's "sanctified." Being "sanctified" also is not just a denomination or a catchy church phrase, it should be a daily process of crucifying the flesh.

> *But in a great house there are not only vessels of*
> *gold and of silver, but also of wood and of earth;*
> *and some to honor, and some to dishonor.*
> *If a man therefore purge himself from these, he shall*
> *be a vessel unto honor, sanctified, and meet for the*
> *master's use, and prepared unto every good work.*
> *2 Timothy 2:20-21*

In this passage of Scripture the word, "sanctified," means, *to make holy, purify* or *consecrate*. A lot of Christians have a desire to be used by God, but Scripture admonishes us to purge ourselves from dishonorable vessels and sanctify ourselves so we *can* be used by God.

The Scripture also reads:

> *Know ye not that the unrighteous shall not inherit*
> *the kingdom of God? Be not deceived: neither*
> *fornicators, nor idolators, nor adulterers, nor effeminate,*
> *nor abusers of themselves with mankind, Nor thieves,*
> *nor covetous, nor drunkards, nor revilers,*
> *nor extortioners, shall inherit the kingdom of God.*
> *And such were some of you: but ye are washed,*
> *but ye are sanctified, but ye are justified in the name*
> *of the Lord Jesus, and by the Spirit of our God.*
> *1 Corinthians 6: 9-11*

Here Paul writes to the Christians at the church in Corinth. He lets them know that they were those things before, but not any more because as Christians, they have been justified by faith in the name of Jesus Christ, who has washed them of their sins because of His shed blood. Because of what Christ did for us on the cross, we have been washed, purified, and sanctified. Because we were once washed, God doesn't want us to return to our former lifestyle, thus making Christ's sacrifice of non effect in our lives.

We don't want to slap God in the face whenever

we lay down with someone we're not married to, even though that is, in essence, what we're doing. God loves us so much that His mercy endures forever and He will forgive us if we confess and repent and turn away, but a lifestyle of sinning and repenting from the same thing over and over again is not what God intends for our lives – it's like a dog returning to its own vomit *(Proverbs 26:11)*.

We cannot move forward in the things of God and receive all the blessings that He has for us if we remain stuck on this issue by not totally surrendering our wills and our bodies to God in this area. Once we surrender all and say, "Yes, Lord," to His will, in every area, then, and only then, can He begin to do a work in us and give us the power and the ability to be kept by Him.

Chapter 5

2 THINGS TO ALWAYS DO WHILE DATING

So now that you understand God's love for you and your mind is renewed so much so that you feel you're ready to date and stay saved, I want you to know that there are two things you should always do, at all times, during the entire dating process.

These two things are watch and pray.

Jesus told His disciples, after He prayed in the Garden of Gethsemane in order to regain strength and courage to fulfill His divine assignment of dying on the cross, to do these two things after He noticed that His disciples had been sleeping instead of praying.

Watch and pray, that ye enter not into temptation:
the spirit indeed is willing, but the flesh is weak.
Matthew 26:41

WATCH

The word, "watch" in *Matthew 26:41* means to keep *awake, watch, be watchful.*

In Webster's Dictionary, 1828 edition, the word, "watch" means *attention; close observation.*

During the dating process, you want to pay close attention to the person you're dating, and observe whether or not he or she has the qualities you're looking for in a mate.

Because it is a good idea to observe whether or not the person has the qualities you're looking for, it would behoove you to have some idea of what you're looking for in a relationship. I believe a lot of people make the mistake of dating the wrong person for years and years because they get to know a person while having no clue about what they're looking for, then eventually decide, 'Nah, he's not the one.' Whereas if you had a better idea, up front, of what you were looking for, then it could have spared you some time and possible heartache.

Comprise a general list of what you're looking for in a mate. No, not a list of 100 things, and no, not shallow items like he has to be six-four or she has to have hazel eyes; jot down what internal, character qualities you're looking for in a spouse.

Now I'm not saying you should date someone you find unattractive. God knows you want to be able to wake up every morning with your spouse and not scream when you look at the person next to you. But just don't be so caught up in the physical. We all have our preferences, but don't cancel a brother or sister in Christ out just because of something shallow that the other person has no control over, such as their height or complexion. In doing so, you may miss out on a major blessing.

For example, on my list, instead of saying brother man has to be as fine as Denzel, I mention that I want him to be pleasing to my sight. In other words, I want him to be cute to me. I realize that my idea of cute is different than a lot of womens' idea of cute, and God knows what I like. Besides, a man with a pure heart towards God, ambition, and a lovable spirit can make a man look fine as wine to me! That's why you don't want to put too much emphasis on physical attributes.

Along with physical attractiveness, you also want to include other qualities that are important to you. I'm not going to sit here and type out your list for you, but I'm sure you have a general idea. For example, do you want someone who is kind-hearted, generous, on the same level spiritually as you are, not only loves God but fears the Lord, is goal-oriented, and slow to anger?

Another suggestion is to examine your past relationships. What did you learn from them? Instead of just coming out of a relationship, learn out of a relationship. What did you learn about yourself from them? What about that other person did you not like, or really got on your nerves? The opposite of what you didn't like about that other person, can then become something you would add to your list of what you're looking for in a mate. Knowing what you're looking for *before* you start dating helps weed out the ones you know wouldn't be a right fit for you.

I also want to mention that you want to make sure that the character qualities you're believing God for a mate are qualities that you, yourself, also currently possess. It's only fair. You don't want to go into a relationship looking for what you can get from that relationship; you want to be able to bring something to the table and be able to give something yourself, more than just how fine you are!

Okay, so now that you have an idea of the qualities you're looking for, now you can observe the qualities within the person you're dating. Again, this is why it's so important to not let on to the person you're dating up front everything you're looking for, instead, you want to observe how they are now. Again, you want to fall in love with the person for who they are as a person, and not just how they treat you.

Pay attention to their behavior, and how they respond to other people, places, things, and situations. Is he or she responsible? Do they pay their bills on time, or are they getting collection calls? If they are getting collection calls, are they cursing out the collector and slamming down the phone? How do they treat other people, besides you? Most people, when they're dating, want to put their best foot forward towards the person their dating, so he may open the door for you, but what about the older lady who comes in behind you? Does he open the door for her, too, or does he just release it on her? That would be rude.

You may meet someone who has all or most of the qualities you're looking for, and they may have extra qualities about them that you enjoy that can be an added bonus! If they don't have every requirement you're looking for on your list, ask yourself if you can tolerate that person not exuding a certain quality. It may not be that they don't have the quality, it may just be that you haven't spent enough time together in order to observe that part of their character. Again, time is always your friend, never your enemy.

ONLY GOD CAN CHANGE SOMEONE

Don't think that if a person doesn't possess a certain quality that you admire that you can change someone into something he's not. You cannot change a man; only God can change someone. So know that while you're dating someone, as you get to know a person over time, realize that what you *watch* and see, is what you get. When you make the decision to accept and continue dating and eventually marry a person, you accept them for who they are, flaws and all, and not for the person you pray that they will one day become.

WATCH THE FRUIT

Wherefore by their fruits ye shall know them.
Matthew 7:20

The Word also says in Matthew 7:17-18, " *Even so every good tree bringeth forth good fruit; but a corrupt tree bringeth forth evil fruit. A good tree cannot bring*

100

forth evil fruit, neither can a corrupt tree bring forth good fruit."

Observe a person's fruit, or what they produce in their lives. Their consistent behavior and lifestyle should be a glimpse as to who they really are. If they do evil things such as lie, cheat, steal, and swear, then that means the fruit is bad and that's who they really are.

What comes out of the fruit of their lips? Do they swear at the drop of a hat, or do they just use the "d" word or the "h" word? Neither is acceptable for a Christian. If the word, "hell," isn't used to describe the place below us then it's being used as a swear word. People who swear and call themselves religious are fooling themselves.

If any man among you seem to be religious,
and bridleth not his tongue, but deceiveth his own
heart, this man's religion is in vain.
James 1:26

Also, if the person you're dating is swearing at situations now, if you decide to marry that person then he or she may curse you out! If you don't swear and are believing God for a mate who doesn't swear as well, and you do not wish to have kids with someone and have them grow up in an environment laden with

101

arguments and swear words, then maybe you shouldn't waste your time dating someone who swears.

Watch their Reputation

Date someone with a good reputation. *Proverbs 22:1 tells us, "A good name is rather to be chosen than great riches, and loving favor rather than silver and gold."*

The word, "name" in this Scripture actually means *character, authority, honor, or fame.*

A person can be famous without ever being on television. Jesus was famous. *Matthew 4:24 says, "And his fame went throughout all Syria: and they brought unto him all sick people that were taken with divers diseases and torments, and those which were possessed with devils, and those which were lunatic, and those that had the palsy; and he healed them."* Before He died and arose, Jesus was famous for healing the sick, preaching the gospel, and teaching the Word of God. Before Jesus even arrived in a certain town, folks knew what His visitation meant, which is why they clamored in droves to get to Him, and even climbed on trees and brought sick friends in beds because they knew that it meant the healer was in the house! Jesus' name meant something.

When it comes to the person you're considering dating, what does their name mean to other people? Does he or she have a good reputation? What do others say about him or her? What do family members say? Does he or she have a good relationship with their family? What do co-workers say? If he takes you to an office party, ask his co-workers, when he's not around, about him and see if they have good things to say. What do church members say at the mention of his name? Along with their verbal response, note their reaction. If they cringe and say, "Brother Marcus? He never gave me that fifty dollars I loaned him three years ago!" then that may not be a good sign. However, on the other hand, if you mention that person's name and someone's eyes light up as they say, "Oh, brother Michael? He's a good brother! He referred me to someone who helped sell my house and he helped me move in. He's a blessing!" Then that may be a good indicator that you may have a gem on your hands.

If the person you're dating has small children, what do his children say about him or her? Kids are so honest, and will tell on you almost every time. Pay attention to what their kids say about them, and really listen to the kids, because if the person is acting fake around you, their kids will tell on them!

WATCH THEIR RELATIONSHIPS
WITH OTHERS

Observe their other relationships besides your own. Ladies, observe his relationship with his family. Does he respect his mother and other female family members? Is he there for them and does he have a good relationship with them? If he doesn't respect others, especially the women in his life, then that may be a good indicator that he may not respect you in the long run. Does he have a good relationship with his father? If his father was absent in his life, does he have any other men around who speak into his life? Does he have mentors, or other male figures that he allows to speak into his life and receive advice from, such as his pastor, or a close friend and confidante?

If he is a father, is he a good one? Does he pay child support on time? Have you observed him paying child support and acknowledging and visiting his child? If you notice that he has children but doesn't acknowledge or take care of them, then that means he's a male but not a man. A man takes care of what he helps bring into this world. A male is just a sperm donor.

Observe who his closest friends are. The saying is true, birds of a feather do flock together, so if his best friend smokes weed every weekend and calls every woman out of her name, then that may be an indicator that your man is putting up a front and hiding his true identity just so he can be with you.

Does he respect authority, or those placed in positions of authority whether it's law enforcement, a judge, or even a teacher? Ask him what well-known or not-so-well-known male figure does he look up to, living or dead, and ask him why he admires this person.

HAVE SOMEONE ELSE *Watch* THE TWO OF YOU!

Sometimes, in relationships, we get so caught up in the moment as we're on cloud nine that we don't always see obvious warning signs. You and your man may be dating and he borrows your car every weekend, verbally abuses you, and always asks you for money, but you may not see it or think by allowing it is just another way to prove to him what a good girlfriend or potential wifey you can be. However, if you tell your closest friend about what's going on in the relationship, she may see it a whole different way. She may be honest and upfront and tell you that he's simply using you for what he can get out of you and that he's not showing you honor or demonstrating his ability to lead in a relationship, which are qualities, ladies, you should look for in a potential mate.

Besides, you don't want to be any man's sugar mama or play thing; you're looking for something serious, right? This is why it's so important to have an accountability partner while dating. Someone you can confide in during the entire dating process. Someone on the outside, looking at, examining, and watching the two of you. It could be a minister, or your best or close friend; someone you trust whom you know wants what's best for you. Someone you don't suspect is jealous of you, but someone who really looks out for you.

One word of caution about the "jealous" thing ladies, not every girlfriend of yours is jealous of you. If you have a boyfriend who is obviously not good for you, and you confide in someone about your relationship and your closest girlfriend tells you the honest truth, then instead of writing her off as, "Oh she just mad 'cuz she ain't got a man," instead, take her words back to the prayer closet and really examine what was said and search within the depths of your soul as to whether or not there is any truth to your friend's observation.

Don't Just Fall in Love with How He Treats You!

Yeah, I said it. I'll say it again. Don't just fall in love with how he treats you! So many women fall into this trap. *"He's so nice, he treats me like a queen, he buys me things, he sent me on a shopping spree, he takes care of my kids . . . "* That may be the case, but you want to observe more than how he treats you. Most men know how to win over a woman. If they see what they want, men are hunters by nature, and they know how to go after what they want. Some of them are so smooth, they know how to say the right things, at the right time, and they know how to listen just enough to bless you with that thing you just said you were believing God for from a conversation six weeks ago. However, you want to observe more than that. How he treats you gives you a taste of what he's capable of, and it may even demonstrate to you that he may care for you, or that he really wants you, but it doesn't say everything about his true character. I've spoken to countless women who said while they were dating, he treated them like royalty, but after they were married he treated them like crap!

You want to observe how he not only treats you, but how he treats others behind closed doors. How does he treat the waitress in the restaurant?

107

Does he go off on her and not leave a tip? That may be an indicator that he has a short temper and is cheap, and just because he may not be that way with you now, doesn't mean he may not treat you that way after you say, "I do." The same goes for men reading this book. Does she treat you like a king, then goes off on someone when she thinks you're not paying attention? Be careful that you don't end up marrying a rooftop woman!

It is better to dwell in a corner of the housetop,
than with a brawling woman in a wide house.
Proverbs 21:9

Instead of being so caught up in how he treats you, grow to admire and respect him for the man he is and the man he has become. Is he genuinely kind to you and others? Does he love God *and* people? Some people get so caught up in "religiosity" that they can praise God one minute in church and curse out their neighbor in the same breath right after they leave service. If they love God, but don't love people, then they don't truly love God.

If a man say, I love God, and hateth his brother, he is
a liar: for he that loveth not his brother whom he hath
seen, how can he love God whom he hath not seen?
1 John 4:20

Is he genuinely a good person? Or is he just a certain way when he is around *you?* Again, a good name is also a good indicator that you may be involved with a good man. So instead of being swept off your feet with how *romantic* he can be, observe and grow to love the true fiber of that man, what's he's made of, and the love of God which is already in him and demonstrated not just to you, but to others as well.

PRAY

The second thing you should always do during the entire dating process is pray. Pray about the person you're dating. I'm not speaking of the shotgun prayer which consists of, "Lord, send me a mate," then you think the next person who comes knocking on your door asking you out must be from God because you just prayed less than a week ago. You want to be careful because when you pray not only does God hear you, but satan hears you, too, and can also send you counterfeits before the real thing shows up. That's why it's so important to watch, and observe that man's fruit to make sure he is truly sent by God.

You want to pray and ask God to show you that man's heart. The Word of God says out of the abundance of the heart, the mouth speaks, so if the person you're dating swears often and condemns others with his words, this may be an indicator that his heart is corrupt. Listen to how he speaks, what he says, and where his heart is concerning money issues, tithing, career and goal-related issues, and family issues. If all of these things are important to you in selecting a mate, then make sure you really listen to how he feels about these issues because it lets you know where his heart is. And once you hear him out first, you can express how you feel as well, but, again, don't expect to change a grown man's mind. Let a person show you who they really are by listening to their words and observing their behavior, then make the decision whether or not this is someone you want to continue to date. The Word of God says in *Luke 8:17, "For nothing is secret that shall not be made manifest; neither any thing hid, that shall not be known and come abroad."* So when you pray to God, you want to ask God to show you the truth about a person, then you want to watch to make sure their actions line up with their words.

Follow Peace - Not a Fleece

As you pray while dating, you also want to make sure you're following peace. Believers today are not to shoot up fleece prayers to God. For example, if a man prays and says, "God, if she's my wife then when I go over and speak to her after church I want her to bat her eyelashes at me three times, flip her hair, then offer me a copy of her notes from today's service. If she does these three things, God, then that means she must be The One!" No, that's not the way it works. A lot of people get this concept from the Old Testament where the servant told God that if the woman comes out to feed her camels, then offers some to his, too, then that must be a sign that she's the one he's been waiting for to introduce to his master to wed *(Genesis 24:12-26)*. The main reason fleece prayers were sent up to God, asking Him to give a sign, is because in the Old Testament, God-fearing people were not saved. They loved God, but Jesus had not died on the cross yet or ascended to heaven yet so He could send another Comforter in the form of the Holy Ghost.

Nevertheless I tell you the truth:
It is expedient for you that I go away:
for if I go not away, the Comforter will

not come unto you; but if I depart,
I will send him to you.
John 16:7

Here Jesus proclaims how it's better for Him to
leave so that The Comforter, known as The Holy
Spirit, can come and live inside the heart of every
born again believer. Prior to Jesus' ascension, Jesus
was confined to wherever He was stationed at the
present moment. Sure, He healed, delivered, and
cast out evil spirits from those He came in contact
with, but once He went away and sent His Spirit,
that same power He used to heal the sick now lives,
resides, and abides on the inside of us!

Howbeit when he, the Spirit of truth, is come, he will
guide you into all truth: for he shall not speak of
himself; but whatsoever he shall hear, that shall he
speak: and he will shew you things to come.
John 16:13

So when you pray about the person you're
dating, ask the Holy Spirit to speak to you about the
other person, and, more importantly, follow peace.
In other words, as you date the person, follow the
peace of God that gives you an inner witness, or an

inward green light of sorts which assures you that it's okay for you to continue in the dating relationship.

YOU'RE NEVER STUCK

Know that with any new dating relationship, there is always a way of escape, and you're never stuck.

If you don't have peace about the person you're dating, and I mean peace from God that this person is the one for you and is truly sent by the Lord, then by all means do not continue in the relationship - no matter how much your flesh doesn't want to break it off because you feel you're so "in love" with the other person.

If, when you pray, you feel led to no longer date the other person, trust that Holy Ghost instinct, or your gut, instead of trusting your own heart because sometimes following your heart instead of following after God's perfect will can get you in a lot of trouble.

For if our heart condemn us, God is greater
than our heart, and knoweth all things.
1 John 2:20

Trust in the Lord with all thine heart; and lean not
unto thine own understanding. In all thy ways
acknowledge him, and he shall direct thy paths.
Be not wise in thine own eyes: fear the Lord,
and depart from evil.
Proverbs 3:5-7

Obey the Holy Ghost Traffic Signal

Consider the spirit man inside you a Holy Ghost traffic signal. When dating someone, with each date, phone conversation, or encounter, pray throughout the entire process. When you pray, listen to your what your spirit is telling you. Don't ignore your inner voice.

I can remember I was in a dating relationship with a gentlemen – the man was so fine, and he was active in church – I just knew he was the one! Well, over time we started "hanging out" at his place. At the time I was also praying to God about my purpose, and I sensed that the gentleman I was seeing wasn't sure about his purpose either. Well, then we started kissing each other, then the next thing you know I'm over there and we're on the couch. The more I hung out with him, the more I discovered there were some character issues about him I wasn't fond of, however I was so caught up in how good it felt kissing him and being around him that I ignored obvious signs of a relationship leading no where.

Well, one night in prayer I felt like God was telling me to cut it off with this man. But rather than flat out tell me to do it, Holy Spirit asked, "*Can* you cut it off?" Even though this man and I never had sex, I was still emotionally attached to him. I didn't want to cut it off! Not wanting to tell that to God, I just cried. Eventually, after a few days I finally gave in and told God "Alright" and cut it off.

Once I finally obeyed God, I kid you not, I received several pages of notes about my purpose and the future that God has for me. This was almost ten years ago, and I remember God's Words and promises being poured out to me like a faucet. I am sure that my obeying God in that one area, which was clogging my ability to clearly hear from God, allowed me to hear from Him once again and receive instructions for my next assignment which, at the time was to attend ministry school, then write my first novel, which went on to be a national bestseller, *He's Fine...But is He Saved?*

Had I ignored the Holy Ghost's red light which told me to stop seeing this man, Lord knows where I would be today. I would probably be somewhere pregnant, or unhappily married. I would probably not have received my purpose, not have written any books (this one is my fourth) and not be able to touch as many lives as I have been blessed to touch if I would have ignored the Holy Ghost traffic signal. But thanks to God's grace, if, at any point in your own life, you ignored God's Holy Ghost warning, know that the Lord is good, and His mercy endures forever, and that as long as you get back on course and surrender this area to God and allow Him to decide who you should and should not date, then He will honor your heart and propel you into your destiny.

Take it Slow

Don't get me wrong; sometimes it's not always a green light or red light. You may meet someone who is saved, and you two may enjoy hanging out with one another, but it's just something deep down on the inside of your spirit that you're not quite sure about with this person. You may not be able to put your finger on it, but for some reason you don't have that green light that's telling you to continue forward in the relationship. In this case, it may not be a green light of *go*, but a yellow light of *take it slow*.

If it's something that you're not quite sure of, don't be afraid to take it slow with the other person, even if it means that you let him know that right now you're led to just be friends with him, but that

116

it doesn't necessarily mean that you're canceling out the opportunity for it to become something more over time.

Honest and open communication throughout the process is key, and involving God in the process by praying to Him and following peace is key as well.

You follow peace when you know the person you're dating adds value to your life and doesn't take away from it or suck the life out of you!

You follow peace when you know the person you're dating motivates and encourages you to follow your dreams, and you the same for them, and that you can see yourselves fitting into each other's future lives together like a hand to a glove.

You follow peace when you pray to God about this person, and there's a warm, peaceful feeling that comes across in your spirit man. Now don't get this confused with the warm fuzzies, no, I'm talking about a peace that passes all understanding.

A peace that let's you know that your hearts are in sync, and your spirits are one.

A peace that confirms that this man is really who he says he is, and loves God more than he loves you.

A peace that shows you that he may be a man after God's heart like David, or a woman of love and sacrifice like Ruth.

You want to follow *that* peace, when you pray, and don't ignore the signs, or the Holy Ghost traffic signal, which is only there to protect you.

Dating on the Phone?

Know that it is possible to date on the phone. Dating on the phone does, indeed, consist of gathering data and information about the other person. This is normally the case when it comes to long distance relationships, because more than likely you talk to the person more than you actually get to visit them. Make sure your conversations are meaningful and that you're collecting data. The only downside to doing too much talking on the phone and not actually going out much is that all you have is what the other person tells you. You don't actually get to really observe their true selves in different public settings and scenarios. You also are not able to interact with his friends, or parents, and find out about his reputation if you're mainly talking on the phone. For these reasons, I would encourage you not to just date on the phone, but also go out on a regular basis in order to observe the person and pray about what you discover.

118

But You Say He's Just a Friend

Also, be careful when speaking to platonic friends on the phone for several hours each day or each week. Sure, the two of you may say you're just friends, but if you're spending so much time with him on the phone, even though you're not spending time with him physically, you're still investing time with him by being on the phone allowing him to use up your time. Between the two of you, though no one said anything is there, one of you may grow attached to the other person and may want to start a relationship. However, if you've already invested so much time with the other person on the phone already, then the relationship may have already started a while ago – you just never gave it a title. Again, I want to encourage you to guard your heart, whenever you spend time with someone, whether in person or on the phone, you are investing in a relationship and it's hard to not allow your heart or true feelings to get involved, no matter how much you say he talks to you about his others "girlfriends." If he cared about them so much, then why is he always on the phone with you?

119

Chapter 6

SEX! IT'S COMPLICATED

Everyone can admit, whether saved or unsaved, that when you introduce sex into a relationship it can complicate things. For instance, lets say a young lady meets a man, they exchange numbers, then "hook up" somewhere, then afterwards he asks her to come to his place, she complies and they end up having sex. Let's say the morning after, she's holding him and they engage in pillow talk followed by a warm exit. She calls him the next day – no answer.

She leaves him a voice mail and he doesn't call back. She sends him a text message, no reply. Next thing you know she's calling him for days and she's still getting thrown into voice mail.

To him, she may have been just a one night stand. He saw her, he wanted her, he got her - next! He's on to the next one to conquer. To her, on the other hand, she may have really liked the guy. She may have thought he was fine, had a nice job, nice house, nice car, and the fact that he approached her and had sex with her somehow led her to believe that she may very well be the one he might think about getting serious with. At least that's what he led her to believe during their pillow talk the morning after as he shared with her his dreams, hopes, and secret fears. During that intimate moment, she actually saw where she could fit into his life and where she could make it all better for him and they could live happily ever after. And the fact that she just gave him her all, in the form of herself, led her to believe that she just might be his soulmate. So now that he's ignoring her, she's angry and bitter at all men in general because she just gave it up to someone she now knows was a complete stranger and she realizes she was nothing but a booty call. Ouch.

We must understand that men and women view sex differently.

For a lot of men, it's physical first, then emotional. Some men see nothing wrong with having sex with a woman while not being emotionally attached. They view it as a physical need being met, which can be met by any willing vessel in the form of the opposite sex. For men, sex can be purely physical – and that's it – they can have sex with a woman for the sheer fun of it without emotional baggage, love, or even affection. There are some men who may later become emotionally attached to the woman he's sleeping with, but there is really no guarantee that this will be the case.

Most women, on the other hand, view sex as emotional first, then physical. Women are more likely to associate sex with love, and quite often have sex with a man hoping and believing it will lead to love. As women we take careful consideration as to who we give ourselves to. Besides, we're allowing another human being to enter inside of us, which should not be taken lightly at all. We're the receivers, while the man is the giver, which was the way God intended.

When we decide to have sex with a man, most of the time it's because we have become emotionally invested in that man, where we believe, at that moment, that he is the best thing since sliced bread so we want to "reward" him by giving ourselves totally and freely to him. If you don't believe me, just ask a married woman whose husband gets on her nerves because he won't take out the trash, or fix anything around the house. If he's getting on her nerves on a regular basis, then more than likely they're not having sex because she ain't giving it up. Not to say this is right, but it's mainly because for women sex is emotional first, then physical.

This is another reason why God intended sex to be within the confounds of marriage, because as two people engage in sex, they become one with each other. The giver and the receiver become one.

> *Therefore shall a man leave his father and*
> *his mother, and shall cleave unto his wife:*
> *and they shall be one flesh*
> *Genesis 2:24*

They become one flesh. The act of sex after marriage seals the covenant. It seals the wedding vows. In the Old Testament the blood was a sign of a covenant, and once a virgin has sex, her hymen is broken, and sometimes there is a shedding of blood, which could also signify the sealing of the marriage covenant. This is the way God intended and the marriage bed is blessed.

So if the marriage bed is blessed, does that mean that the bed shared by two unmarried people is cursed? Yes! As mentioned in Chapter 4, sex outside of God's will defiles the temple of God. However, we must realize that a oneness still takes place, but it's definitely not the kind of oneness that God intended. A oneness takes place which could result in a curse from disobeying God and His commandments (*Deuteronomy 28:15-19*) and it also gives satan access to your life.

The Word of God says that the wages of sin is death (*Romans 6:23*). The word "wages" means paycheck, so the paycheck for a lifestyle of sin is death. It could mean catching an STD such as AIDS/HIV which would eventually lead to a physical death. Folks are crying about "why aren't black people getting tested for AIDS?" Well the answer is clear as day, why should you get tested for something where you know there is a 50/50 chance that, if you're sexually active, you may very well have it? The answer is because folks are AFRAID! They'd rather not know, avoid getting tested, so they won't have to alter their life and then become accountable to the fact that a promiscuous lifestyle has led them down this path. Don't get me wrong, I believe you *should* get tested, but once you get tested and find out you test negative for HIV (because of the grace of God) then I propose you then remain abstinent until marriage (and that you and your fiance' both get tested before you say, "I do") so that way you won't have to *fear* the possibility of contracting the deadly disease.

There is not only the possibility of dying physically because of sin's paycheck, you could also die emotionally. As I tour across the country, spreading the "abstinence until marriage" message, I cannot tell you how many times women have told me that they wish they had waited before they had sex. Whether it was peer pressure as a teenager, a longing for what they believed to be love, or simply because their body was craving that other man, they all say that if they could do it over again, they would not have given themselves up to someone else. Besides, who wants to give up total control of one's own body, and give someone you barely know – your very essence and your very being in the form of your body? No woman I know had sex with someone knowing that after they had sex they would break up a couple months later. No one! Why? Because that's not how God intended for it to be.

He did not intend for us to become one with ten different men then break covenant, and break covenant, and on to the next one, and on to the next one. In a sense it's just like we're practicing divorce before we're even married!

This continued practice can lead to emotional hardship and may cause you to not trust any man, thereby giving the one truly good brotha who wants to purposefully date you a hard time because you're so used to being used and then thrown away! God wants us to be whole and complete in Him.

And ye are complete in him, which is the head
of all principality and power.
Colossians 2:10

Ladies, we must realize that we don't need a man to "complete us" despite what those song lyrics say, and we don't need a man to be inside us, holding and caressing us in order for us to feel loved. The only man we should allow to come inside of us before we're married is our Heavenly Father, and after He does come inside our hearts, at least we won't have to worry about catching an STD or getting pregnant!

SEX PUTS THE BLINDERS ON

Sex outside of marriage complicates things also because it can be very emotional for some once they've given it up, especially women, as it puts the relationship "blinders" on. You know what I mean, that man may be no good for you. Your momma, your daddy, your sister, your brother, your best friend, *everybody* may be telling you that man is no good for you, but because he's so good in bed, you ignore everyone else's rational thinking because you feel like no man on this green earth can make you feel the way your man makes you feel and that he must be the one.

What you may not realize, is that the only reason you feel so strongly about this man is not because he treats you like a queen - you know that there have been days he treated you like crap, like when he threw you out of his car and left you to fend for yourself and find your own way home, or when he cursed you out in front of your child, or when he beat you 'til your face turned black and blue, you *know* he ain't right – but because he's so good in bed and says the right things and knows how to work it the right way, then you try and justify being blind to the truth.

The truth is, if he's going to treat you like less of a woman, or even less of a human being, then no, he doesn't love you, no matter how many things he buys you and no matter how much he tells you about how monogamous he is with you and only you. If he really loved you, then he would value you and your decision to wait until you're married before the two of you have sex. He wouldn't leave you at the drop of a hat once you told him. If he did then that's just proof that he doesn't really love you anyway but was more concerned about what he could get *from* you sexually.

For me, personally, once I tell men I'm a virgin and that I'm savin' it until marriage, that is a perfect "weeder" to let me know what guys are truly serious about getting to know me for the purpose of dating which could lead to marriage, and those who just saw an attractive face and a nice body they wanted to conquer and get in bed. My firm conviction and firm stance on this issue may have cost me some dates or nights on the town with some cute guys, but I'm at the point where I don't have time for foolishness. If you're so *saved*, then you would not only respect my wishes, but would also strive to live an abstinent, saved lifestyle yourself.

So beware of the blinders, which is why it's best not to give it up to the person you're dating so those blinders don't even have the opportunity to come on in the first place. You don't want to fool yourself into thinking you really love someone when really it's their bedroom performance that you truly love. To some of you reading this book who have been sexually active in the past, if you think about your last relationship and took sex out of the equation, you may discover that there wasn't much else there.

This is not to say all men are dogs and that they're only after one thing. There are some good ones out there. I've also spoken to men who do view sex as an emotional event, and they find themselves "wide open" to a woman who they may have truly cared about, had sex with on more than one occasion, only to discover that she may have been using him for his money, or thought he was a "softey" so she ended up getting her a little something on the side.

Society may call this man, "whipped," but there is nothing wrong with being "whipped" as long as you're being whipped by your spouse! All the emotions and the connection formed by the person you have sex with are what God meant to create the oneness that cannot be broken but is meant to be shared between husband and wife. It is when we get outside of God's will and have sex as single believers do we end up with the spiritual, physical, or emotional damage that comes along with creating a oneness with someone who God did not intend for us to become one with in the first place!

Sex within the confounds of marriage is the ultimate act of love that you can demonstrate towards your spouse.

Real love is not an emotion, it's an action. Once you're married, you celebrate your love for one another each time you have sex. God so loved, that He gave. You so love, so you give yourself to your spouse. As a single believer, you so love God, first, that you give your body to Him, as a living sacrifice, before you give yourself away to your spouse.

As a single believer, one of the ways we glorify God, more than with shouts of praise through our lips on Sunday morning, is with our bodies.

For ye are bought with a price:
therefore glorify God in your body,
and in your spirit, which are God's.
1 Corinthians 6:20

We glorify God in our spirits when we pray, worship, and praise God. We glorify God in our bodies when we make a decision to become abstinent until marriage, then we walk it out.

DON'T RUN FROM GOD – ALWAYS RUN TO GOD

Sex outside of marriage for believers brings shame, because if it's not done in the will of God then the first thing a believer wants to do is run and hide from God. For example, look at Adam and Eve. When Adam and Eve sinned against God by partaking of the forbidden fruit, the Bible said their eyes were opened and they realized they were naked so they attached fig leaves to their bodies to cover

131

themselves. They then tried to hide from God and deny any wrongdoing.

And they heard the voice of the Lord God walking in the garden in the cool of the day: and Adam and his wife hid themselves from the presence of the Lord God amongst the trees of the garden.
Genesis 3:8

Adam and Eve heard God's voice in the area, but instead of fessing up to their sin, or their mistake, they tried to hide from an all-knowing, all-seeing Omniscient God.

And the Lord God called unto Adam, and said unto him, Where art thou? And he said, I heard thy voice in the garden, and I was afraid, because I was naked; and I hid myself.
Genesis 3:9-10

Here Adam is still trying to cover up his and Eve's sin by claiming He was hiding from God because he didn't want God to see him naked. God next asks him how does he know he's naked, then Adam starts playing the blame game by telling God that the woman *He* gave him *made* him eat the forbidden fruit. So not only was Adam trying to run away from his sin, he was also in self-denial trying to blame others for his own mistake.

A lot of times, as believers, if we miss God or get outside of the will of God by practicing an unrepentant promiscuous lifestyle, or trying to "party like a rock star" every week, the first thing we want to do is run away from God. We stop going to church as much, we stop fellowshipping with other believers, and we stop praying like we used to. As this continues, we eventually become what the Bible calls a backslidden Christian (Jeremiah 8:5). However, we must know that as believers we never have to be at a place where we feel we can never be honest with God about everything, including our feelings, our mistakes, or when we miss it.

As far as Adam and Eve, God knew they partook of the forbidden fruit. God knows everything. However, God still asks Adam whether or not he ate it in *Genesis 3:11* when He says, *"...Who told thee that thou wast naked? Hast thou eaten of the tree, whereof I commanded thee that thou shouldest not eat?"* Here was Adam's opportunity to tell the truth. But instead, Adam blamed Eve for his mishap.

How many times do we miss it, or fall into sexual sin over and over again, and blame others such as the woman who "threw herself at me" or the man who, *"said* he was saved" or sometimes folk even blame God by saying, "God, *you're* the one who gave me all this sperm and all this testosterone, what am I supposed to do with it?" instead of going to God, sincerely repenting, and asking God to help you stay strong and remain abstinent until marriage.

This is not to say that you'll never make a mistake. Nobody is perfect, and we all miss it at times. If anyone says they never missed God or never sinned or made a mistake then know that that person is lying *(1 John 1:8)*. The most important thing that God examines is the heart.

If you have a heart to serve and please God and do not wish to break His heart by having sex outside of marriage, then God honors your heart. If you miss it and slip up and sleep with someone you're not married to and had no intentions on sleeping with that person, if you truly and sincerely repent before God then God will honor your prayer and cleanse you from all wrongdoing.

Come now, and let us reason together, saith
the LORD: though your sins be as scarlet, they
shall be as white as snow; though they be red like
crimson, they shall be as wool.
Isaiah 1:18

I can remember a time when I seemingly kept missing it time after time again. I was involved in a relationship with another Christian, and though we never had sex, sometimes I would stop by his place and we'd end up kissing or making out.

Please be advised, just because we didn't "go all the way," didn't make it right in the sight of God. I was still allowing someone else to utilize my body in an unholy way which was not pleasing to God. I knew I shouldn't have been doing it, but at the time I just felt like I just couldn't resist. My flesh couldn't resist and it would often give in.

However, after I would visit this man, I would go home feeling like a wreck. As a twenty-something-year-old at the time, I would go to my mom's back porch and just cry out to God, repent, and God would then minister to me and speak to my heart. It seemed like each time He would lead me to the same passage of Scripture:

Let not sin therefore reign in your mortal body, that
ye should obey it in the lusts thereof. Neither yield ye
your members as instruments of unrighteousness unto
sin: but yield yourselves unto God, as those that are
alive from the dead, and your members as

> *instruments of righteousness unto God.*
> *For sin shall not have dominion over you: for ye are*
> *not under law, but under grace.*
> *Romans 6:12-14*

Even though I felt like I kept being led to the same Scripture, over and over again, God was encouraging me not to allow sin to have rule and reign over my body. Our bodies are instruments, and the word, "instrument," in Webster's Dictionary means, *That which is subservient to the execution of a plan or purpose, or to the production of an effect; means used or contributing to an effect; applicable to persons or things.* So, in essence, I was using my body as an instrument of sin, and the only purpose and plan of sin is eventually death *(Romans 6:23)*.

Though it felt good to the flesh, I was treading upon satan's territory every time I yielded my members as instruments of unrighteousness, and, as stated before, satan's plan and purpose for the believer, or for anyone for that matter, is to steal, kill, and destroy *(John 10:10)*.

The Lord continued to minister to me, and led me to the next passage of Scripture as well:

> *Know ye not, that to whom ye yield yourselves*
> *servants to obey, his servants ye are to whom ye obey;*

whether of sin unto death,
or of obedience unto righteousness?
Romans 6:16

In other words, God was telling me that whoever I yielded myself to, or yielded my members to, I became that person's servant and they then become my master. So here I was allowing some other man to handle me and hold me as I yielded my members to him, even though with my lips I would say on Sunday morning that God was my Master.

A son honoureth his father, and a servant
his master: if then I be a father, where is mine honour?
And if I be a master, where is my fear?...
Malachi 1:6

Whatever relationship you're involved in with someone, you want it to be one that causes you to grow in your relationship with God, not one that takes you away from God or has you at the altar repenting seemingly every Sunday morning.

I can honestly say that I found the strength and confidence to break off that relationship because, even though I kept missing it time and time again, I kept running *to* God, instead of away *from* God. I would cry out to God, repent with the intention of not making the same mistake again, and if I missed it again, I would repent again. God still loved me, and He welcomed me with open arms each time I came to Him. I asked for His forgiveness, and He washed my sin away because of the shed blood of Jesus.

As believers we must never forget about the power of the blood of Jesus.

It is because of Jesus' shed blood which was presented to the mercy seat when Jesus ascended into heaven that you and I can go to God with boldness when we pray, and know that when we sincerely repent before God after missing the mark, that God will wash away our sins every time.

If we confess our sins, he is faithful and just
to forgive us our sins, and to cleanse
us from all unrighteousness.
1 John 1:9

So if we've been cleansed of unrighteousness because of the shed blood of Jesus, then what's left? Righteousness. And once God washes our sins away, then we, immediately after we acknowledge and repent each time before God, are brought back in right fellowship with God and are back to being made the righteousness of God.

For he hath made him to be sin for us,
who knew no sin; that we might be made the
righteousness of God in him.
2 Corinthians 5:21

It's the grace of God that keeps us, and it's the power of His grace that we can run to Him if we ever miss it, instead of running away from Him, knowing that He hears us, He loves us, and that He wants to be with us more than anything in the world.

As I mentioned in the first chapter of this book, more than anything God wants to have fellowship with us. We were created to have an 'in love' relationship with God. Just like we wouldn't want our spouse to just throw us away or leave us if we made a mistake, God doesn't want us to run from Him if we make a mistake. Instead, He wants us to run to Him every time.

He's not like a judge ready to strike you down with lightening the minute you make a mistake. No, He' s like the father of the prodigal son, who was ready to receive with open arms his backslidden son who had gone astray *(Luke 15:11-32).*

So even if you have had sex in the past, the fact that you have read this much of this book shows God that you are serious about wanting to know how to get it right in this area of your life. If you repent to God, right now, out loud as you pray only to Him, and ask Him to forgive you of your past sexual behavior, He will forgive you, and He will cleanse you, and you will be cleansed on the inside and made as pure as white snow.

NOT GUILTY!

Believe that He has forgiven you and believe His Word when it says,

My little children, these things write I unto you, that ye sin not. And if any man sin, we have an advocate with the Father, Jesus Christ the righteous.
1 John 2:1

The word "advocate" means, to *plead in favor of or to defend by argument.* So in a court of law satan stands as the accuser of the brethren, where you may have missed God and had sex outside of marriage fifty-seven times. When satan tells you that you're unworthy of forgiveness, and then tells God, who sits as the Judge, that you'll never amount to anything and that the only thing you're good for is to be had in bed, know that at that very moment your advocate, Jesus, will approach the bench and stand before God to plead in your favor and defend your argument by saying, "This, my child, stands before you in this court. She has sincerely confessed her sin, and I shed My blood for her on the cross over 2,000 years ago for all of her sins, and because she honored Your Word, Your Honor, found in *1 John 1:9*, then I say that she be found innocent of any wrongdoing." Then at that very moment our great Judge in court, God, renders a verdict, slams his gavel and proclaims, "Not Guilty!"

So no matter what your past may have looked like, don't listen to the enemy's lies, believe what God says about you, and know that if He has forgiven you, then you're forgiven – period. It's through grace that we are saved through faith, and not of ourselves – it is the gift of God *(Ephesians 2:8)*. It's because of God's grace that we can confess our sins, repent – which meants to turn away, and pray to our God so that we can be free to stand before Him cleansed, healed, and whole again.

GO, AND SIN NO MORE

So because God is such a loving and forgiving God, it is so important that you learn to forgive yourself. Learn to forgive yourself for getting involved with men who just used you and didn't bother to call you back the next day. Learn to forgive yourself for believing others' lies and manipulative tactics that ended up landing you in bed. Forgive yourself for having sex out of wedlock which may have produced an offspring – remember that it's not the child's fault and that life, itself, is a blessing from God even though it may not have been conceived in ideal circumstances. Forgive yourself, and move on.

God said as far as the east is from the west, so far hath He removed our transgressions from us *(Psalm 103:12)*. The east and west never meet, which means God does not remember our past sins at all.

There has never been a time where I prayed to God and He brought up a mistake I made last year, last week, or even yesterday. He always speaks to me about being His loving daughter, and He always ministers to me about the work He would have me to do for Him, in spite of my past sins which He no longer recalls because I immediately ask for forgiveness as soon as I make a mistake.

So because God no longer remembers our past sins, then you should not remember your past sins either. The Word of God says in *Hebrews 10:2 "... the worshippers once purged should have had no more conscience of sins."* As believers we are to no longer even be conscious of our past sins. Our past mistakes and sins shouldn't even cross our minds anymore once we repent. Don't even think about them. Don't allow the enemy to whisper lies in your ear by telling you how you are a bad, unworthy person and how God doesn't love you and that you'll never stand a chance of catching a good man because you've been used so much in the past. Remember that satan is the father of lies *(John 8:44)*, so recognize that anything he tells you is a complete lie.

As long as you have been made a child of God, then you are precious in the sight of God; you're so valuable to God that if you were the only person on this earth, God still would have sent His Son, Jesus, to die for you *(John 3:16)*.

Believe what God says about you, that you are more than a conqueror *(Romans 8:37)*,
that though your sins were as scarlet, they shall be as white as snow *(Isaiah 1:18)*, and that you are God's workmanship, created in Christ Jesus unto good works *(Ephesians 2:10)*.

Keep your past mistakes washed away under the blood, forgive yourself, forgive those who may have hurt you or broke your heart, and move on. Move forward, committing to God, starting this day, to remain abstinent and whole until your wedding night.

Chapter 7

5 Ways To Intimacy Without Sex

I can remember a time years ago during a question and answer segment at a singles event, a lady asked the question, "If you're not having sex in a relationship, then what do you *do* as a couple?" Some people in the audience snickered at her question, but I heard her heart and knew that it took a lot of guts for her to get up in front of a ton of people and ask that question. Her question led me to believe that there may be many like her, who sincerely love God, but just don't know what to do as a substitute for sex while in a loving relationship with another person. Some may not know of any other way to express sincere love for the person that they're dating or are in love with. Which leads me to this chapter – this chapter will give five ways you can express sincere love for the person you're dating – without having sex. True intimacy *can* be attained without exchanging body heat.

The word, "intimacy" broken down is, "into-me-see." As your dating relationship progresses and trust is established, you eventually allow the other person to see "into" your heart, "into" your soul, "into" your dreams, and vice versa.

One of the ways you express love for someone else is when you both verbally share each others dreams, desires, and goals – dreams that only few know about. Love can be taken a step further when the person you're dating becomes actively involved in helping make your dreams come true. Whether it's praying with and for you, attending events and helping out as a show of support, letting others know about what you're working on and enlisting help or assisting you – all these actions demonstrate love for the other person. The other person doesn't *have* to do it, no one has to help you in whatever you're working on, so the fact that they're willing to help shows that they are unselfishly inviting themselves into your world where you desire to realize your own aspirations, hopes, and dreams – as you do the same for them.

LOVE WITH YOUR WORDS

Another way to express love is through speaking words of life and encouragement over one another. The world is so filled with negative people – you walk down the street and folks barely want to speak to each other; you're on the job and your boss gets on your nerves; or you don't feel like yet another day of hearing co-workers gossip and bad mouth one another; you go home and turn on the news and you hear bad reports about the economy. Sometimes it gets to a point where all you're hearing is negativity and bad news over and over again. How much more of a joy would it be, then, to have the person you're dating speak words of life and encouragement, hope, and plans for a brighter future over you in the midst of it all?

Words of affirmation, such as compliments and encouragement, communicate love. As you speak to your significant other, you want to build them up and not bury them with your words. Words can either cut sharp like a dagger, or be as sweet as a honeycomb – you want to strive for the latter.

Pleasant words are as an honeycomb,
sweet to the soul, and health to the bones.
Proverbs 16:24

Just like God's Word is filled with life and hope, when a Christian couple speak words of life, hope and encouragement over one another, it lets the other person know that there is someone who believes in them and is on their side – no matter what may be going on in the outside world. Encouraging one another verbally is a way to express love for someone, because it motivates them to be the best woman or man of God whom God has already predestined him or her to be.

Let no corrupt communication proceed out of your
mouth, but that which is good to the use of edifying,
that it may minister grace unto the hearers.
Ephesians 4:29

A lot of times, the way you speak to someone may determine whether or not the person will continue dating you. As the saying goes, it's not what you say, it's how you say it. No matter how justified you may feel in your response, you don't want to scare your date away because you've communicated in a way that comes off as explosive or demeaning.

148

Speak kind words, speak the truth in love, and allow the fruit of the Spirit in the form of gentleness and temperence to take root in you as you become that Proverbs 31:26 person whose words are full of wisdom and the law of kindness.

DO UNTO OTHERS . . .

A third way of showing love is by acts of kindness, or doing nice things for the other person. Whether it's bringing lunch to them on their job, or giving them a ride to church if their car is in the shop, consistent small acts of kindness lets the other person know that you truly care for them. Now don't get it twisted, ladies, I'm not talking about going over that man's house every weekend to fix his dinner, wash his feet, and do his laundry. Now that's a bit much, and you don't want the man to get most of the benefits of being married without him even putting a ring on it, but I'm just saying do little things which show that you're thinking about the other person, and that you love them – without having sex.

It's the Thought That Counts

A fourth way to express love is to give each other gifts. Hold up! I'm not talking about expensive, lavish gifts like a new car or diamond necklace. As the saying goes, it's the thought that counts. For instance, man of God, if you know your woman of God is studying to be a fashion designer, then you can purchase a subscription to her favorite fashion magazine, or purchase tickets to a fashion show that the two of you can attend together. Of course she would know that you spent money on the gifts, but it also lets her know that you're taking an interest in what she's interested in and is willing to be there for her – even if you, yourself, aren't that much into fashion.

Time Well Spent

A final, and fifth way to express love for someone is to spend quality time with the person you're dating, simply by being there. When a loved one makes his or her transition to heaven, or when a relative gets rushed to the hospital, you want to be that person who is there for the person you're dating. You want to be there during certain, important life events including graduations, awards banquets, holidays, or birthday parties.

Spending time with the other person doesn't mean being stuck at one's place alone where the temptation to have sex may be too much for the two of you to bear, instead you can spend quality time together doing things you both enjoy. You can compromise each week, meaning one weekend you do something one person likes and the next weekend you do something the other person likes. It helps if your interests are similar, but realistically that may not always be the case. For example, it's okay if the two of you have different tastes in music, just so long as you both respect each other's tastes and choose to enjoy what you both enjoy as you go out, because it's about spending time with one another – not the actual activity itself.

By utilizing one if not all five of these ways to express sincere love for the person you're purposefully dating, you may be pleased to discover that true intimacy can be attained and a loving relationship can be formed without having sex. In doing so, you may also determine that this person may eventually hold a special place in your heart and may one day fill it as your lifelong partner, future lover, true confidant, and best friend.

Chapter 8

TESTIMONIALS —
THESE COUPLES DID IT!

These Christian couples did it. They dated for at least a year and remained abstinent during the entire dating process until marriage. The couples represented in these examples represent different walks of life, different age groups, and different experiences. Some of them were both virgins, or maybe one was and the other wasn't, or maybe both weren't. What they all have in common, though, is their decision to remain abstinent while dating one another until after they said, "I do." It *is* possible to make it to the altar before the bedroom. Read about how these couples did it, and know that you can, too, if you put your mind and heart to it. With God, all things are possible!

Dennis and Lonnica Crawford
You're Gonna Love Me!

D ennis initially laid eyes on his wife in 1994 as she was on stage belting the lyrics of Jennifer Holiday's, "And I Am Telling You." And as a backslidden Christian man at the time watching Lonnica sing and sway put him in a trance! They were college friends and were dating different people at the time, however God brought them back in each other's paths as Dennis joined a new church in 1998 and Lonnica joined that same church the same year. No longer dating, however

Dennis, 36, and Lonnica, 35, with (l to r) James and Caleb of Warren, MI

seeking God and having his relationship with God

154

restored, Dennis began to notice Lonnica even more. "God began to put her on my heart," he recalls.

He approached her to date in 1999, however Lonnica told him 'no' for almost four months before agreeing to go out with him. Unbeknownst to Dennis, he pursued her while she was getting healed emotionally after cutting off a prior engagement in which the Lord told her not to marry the person. Though she liked Dennis, Lonnica didn't want to take him through her own healing process, which was why she kept turning him down.

However Jennifer Holiday's song title must have resonated in Dennis's soul because he refused to give up. He had an inward witness from the Lord that Lonnica was his wife and he had eyes for no one else.

She finally agreed to go out with him and they started dating in 1999 and were married almost two years later.

In spite of their pasts, Dennis and Lonnica "stayed saved" with each other by discussing the expectation of remaining abstinent with each other beforehand, holding hands, and by not being out with each other at night and by being accountable to another married Christian couple. Dennis also said he loves his wife's feet and asked her not to wear open-toed shoes around him so in the summertime Lonnica didn't wear open-toe sandals so as to not be a stumbling block to her future Boaz.

Lonnica encourages single women who are

believing God for a mate to, "Run after God and ask God to prepare you for your mate so you can be the best help meet for him and have a tight relationship with God first so you don't get into a relationship and then forget God."

In regards to advice for single men, Dennis says, "I come across a lot of single brothers that are like sex, sex, sex, sex, sex, because we're very visual, but what I tell them is, 'get yourself together spiritually because you're going to be the leader (of the home) and that woman's (spiritual) covering so you are held more accountable spiritually so get your heart right before God. Have an attitude of servanthood and also get your finances tight because when you marry a woman of God, she wants security – she wants to know that you got her spiritually, physically and financially and just make sure you're not settling by compromising yourself and compromising your body just so you can have sex.'"

*Dennis is the author of, **Heart Meditation of the Believer**,*
and is currently a Federal Employee.
Lonnica is a Home Manager, Realtor and Event Specialist/
Business Partner of Exquisite Designs Event Planning, LLC

Carl and April Williams
Patience Prevails

April just knew she was going to be married by 22. She had no idea that by her 30th birthday, and even years after that, she would still be unmarried. However, as she patiently waited on God, she refused to compromise what she was believing God for in a mate. Similarly, Carl thought he was ready to be married at 30. Seven years later, after a string of dating 'wrong ones' he, too, wondered what was the hold up.

Then on that glorious day in 2007, Carl met April amongst a group of friends at church.

Carl admits to not having a lightning bolt from heaven strike him down and

Carl, 40, and April, 37, of Detroit, MI

say, "This is God. April is your wife." They dated two years and during that time they spent a lot of time getting to know each other. Carl liked the fact that April served in the church as he did, but he wanted to observe how she responded outside the church and make sure, "she was who she said she was," he recalls.

They 'stayed saved' with each other during the dating process by discussing, up front, their abstinence expectation. They also knew their limits, and April recalls they would even 'put each other out' with no need of explanation if they knew they were at a point where the temptation to slip in the bedroom got a little too hard for them to bear. Also, the fact that they prayed that they would be an example to other Christian couples of how to do it God's way kept them off of each other.

Carl recommends that all Christian couples who are seriously dating read and discuss with each other these three books: *His Needs, Her Needs,* by Willard F. Harley, *Love and Respect,* by Emerson Eggerichs, and, *The Five Love Languages,* by Gary Chapman.

When April was asked what advice she has for single women believing God for a mate, particularly those over 30, she says, "Don't compromise what you ask God for, and have patience. Don't listen to people who tell you what you can't have because you reach a certain age – it's okay to believe God for a mate who doesn't have kids if that's what you want. And don't put your life on hold while waiting for someone to come along, hang around with single saved friends who can lift you up."

Carl Williams is a radiographer and
April Williams is a social worker.

Aurelio and Michelle McQueen
First Baby at 42

Aurelio and Michelle initially met in church at an auxiliary meeting and Michelle, 30 at the time, fondly remembers saying to herself, "Ask me out, ask me out!" upon first meeting him. Well he didn't give her his phone number that day, however, after running into each other on a different occasion and waving "hello" to each other at other auxiliary meetings, it eventually led to a two year friendship.

Aurelio, 38, and Michelle, 42, with Alexander Christopher of Farmington Hills, MI

During that time, Aurelio explained how he was totally focused on God at that time and wasn't interested in a dating relationship, while Michelle prayed with five other ladies who were all believing God for a mate. Michelle wasn't necessarily praying that Aurelio be 'the one' but she was praying that God would send her mate and felt that God was preparing her for marriage.

"In 2000, the Lord started dealing with me about getting married and stuff like that," Aurelio admits. The same year Michelle prayed with her friends, Aurelio made it known to her that he was interested in dating her.

Aurelio and Michelle dated and remained abstinent during the entire three years that they dated.

When asked how did they do it, Michelle says, "My roommate and I made a pact with each other that we wouldn't let any men in our apartment. She was my accountability."

Aurelio and Michelle also served together at church, were not at each other's apartment at night, dated with other couples, dated in public such as the movies and enjoyed walks in the park. Michelle mentioned how some days they would just walk and talk by the water at Erma Henderson Park in Detroit. "That was attractive to me," Michelle says. "It made me more attracted to him by just listening to the wisdom that came out of him, his vision and the goals and dreams that he had."

They married in 2003 and at this writing of this are enjoying their six-month old baby boy, Alexander Christopher McQueen. Michelle had him at the age of 42, after miscarrying at 40. Doctors told her that she miscarried because of her age and asked her if she would consider using donor eggs. However Michelle refused and instead chose to believe God, along with her husband, as they held strong to their faith, had hands laid on them at their church, and that same year Michelle gave birth to a 9 lb baby boy.

Aurelio advises single men: "Know that the steps of a good man are ordered by the Lord and everything that you need and desire is in the path that God has you walking in and as you continue you may run right into your spouse. You want to know for a fact that the person you're dating is from God for you because a woman can determine the rise and fall of a man and if you marry the wrong woman it could be like hell on earth. Check with God on every aspect. It's not easy, but it's safe."

Michelle advises single women: "Enjoy where you are in the season you're in. Enjoy the moment instead of constantly looking ahead. It's nothing wrong with praying and believing God for a mate. God says He will give you the desires of your heart so if that's the case, God knows where you are and He knows where the man is, but in the meantime, He has a work for you to do right now."

Aurelio is a facility engineer for a food management company and Michelle McQueen is a relocation consultant for a real estate company.

Royce and Andrea Hart
When Purpose and Lifelong Love Collide

Andrea was on a journey of a lifetime after having completed ministry school and now off to a "foreign land," so to speak to help in the ministry. Little did she know that in doing so, on a voyage from Farmington Hills, MI to Jacksonville, FL, that she would meet and marry her husband shortly thereafter.

Andrea first met Royce in 2005 at a leadership meeting for home Bible study fellowships established by their church. Their friendship led to their dating relationship which caused Royce to realize Andrea was his wife.

Royce, 30, and Andrea, 30, of Jacksonville, FL

"When I met Andrea, I wasn't interested in dating anybody at all," Royce admits, "I was just going to dedicate all my time and efforts to the Lord. I was five years abstinent so I wasn't about to jump into any relationship and have that compromised." However, once he met Andrea it was her virtuous character and helpfulness that stood out to him.

Royce realized Andrea was his wife throughout the dating process once he understood that though a lot of their interests weren't that similar, their callings were complementary to one another. Royce says, "You know you have a help meet when they can help you in an area where you're lacking and vice versa."

At the start of their dating relationship, Andrea, a twenty-seven year old virgin at the time, sat down with Royce and discussed how their relationship was going to look. They both agreed premarital sex was out of the question.

Andrea advises Christian couples to always keep God at the head of the relationship and any time you notice your time with God or your intimacy with God slipping, then you need to reevaluate and ask yourself if the relationship is really of God.

She advices single women, "Continue to live your life in expectation of getting a mate, but don't let that expectation drive your life, in other words enjoy your singleness, enjoy your life as it is now and let that man come and add to what you already have going on. Let yourself be an asset and not so much a liability. As you're walking out your purpose...He's just going to bring this person along because it's part of walking out God's divine destiny for your life."

Royce Hart is founder & CEO of AGAPE Clothing Company,
www.myagapelife.com.
Andrea I. Hart is founder & executive director of
Virtuous Excellence Personal Development, Inc.and
author of Kept: Preserved for Purpose
www.andreaihart.com

Kevin and Angela Cobb
Restoration After Divorce

Kevin was married before in 1995. In 1998 he suffered the pain of divorce and called it, "the worst thing that could ever happen to me in my entire life." He told himself, "I'm through with women." He didn't trust them anymore, he couldn't believe a word they said. He figured there were some disciples in the Bible who were single, so he may as well be like one of them. He was content with just himself and his Bible and was just focused on making it to heaven.

Then he met Angela.

Angela and Kevin were both active members of the same church for well over ten years. They were introduced to one another prior to dating and a female ministry leader asked Angela, "What about Cobb?" and she initially replied, "He's not my type." Also, Angela was just grieving the loss of her mother so she really wasn't ready to date anyone.

Then one day in 2000, members of their church

attended a single's ministry conference in Cincinnati, OH and afterwards grabbed a bite to eat and discussed heading to the a m u s e m e n t park afterwards. I n t e r e s t i n g l y enough, both Kevin and Angela weren't fond of amusement

Kevin, 39, Angela, 41, with children (l to r) Kaitlin, Karrington, and Kevin II of Detroit, MI

parks, so Kevin asked Angela if she'd like to go to lunch, followed by a walk around the city instead. Angela agreed, and in her words, "We've never been apart since that day."

During their two year dating experience, they prayed together, studied the Word together, and worshipped together as they sat next to each other every Sunday. They also served alongside each other in whatever capacity whether it was on the administrative team at church, coat drives, fundraising for missions, or leading a Bible discussion at a local Starbucks.

Though Angela was abstinent ten years before dating Kevin, she admitted that dating at 34 produced its own set of challenges so she wanted to make sure she didn't fall into sexual sin by surrounding herself and remaining accountable to other women in the ministry.

Kevin had made up in his mind that premarital sex was not an option because he described his dating experience with his previous marriage as worldly and anything but godly so he wanted to do it God's way this time and was looking forward to him and Angela experiencing sex with each other for the first time on their wedding night.

Kevin and Angela dated and "stayed saved" by planning all their dates (i.e., no one just 'showed up' at the other's house or apartment unannounced), double dating - sometimes even with the married couple who was to lead them in premarital counseling, and not being out with each other's place late at night.

Angela and Kevin became so inseparable that they married in 2002 and had their first child together in 2003, their second in 2005, and at age 40, Angela gave birth to their third child in 2007.

Kevin Cobb works in customer service and Angela Cobb is a teacher.

Moeski and Nicki Lynch
Long Distance Love

Moeski and Nicki Lynch first met at a mutual friend and fellow church member's birthday party. He introduced himself to her along with other ladies at the party and discovered that Nicki was also a member of the church he attended. During their initial encounter, Moeski jokingly said he would then start seeing Nicki at church more often and sure enough his prophetic words came to pass.

Moeeski asked Nicki out just before she was soon to head back to her home town of Atlanta. As they got to know each other, they discovered that they had similar passions and complementary callings. Moeski was known as charming jokester, which was why it took Nicki a minute to take him seriously. However, she

Moeski, 31, and Nicki Lynch, 34, of Sarasota, FL

eventually discovered that he did have a sincere

heart for God, and that he was actively pursuing his calling as a screenwriter, television and film producer – which complemented her passion for web design and multimedia.

Once Nicki left for Atlanta, they did not let their distance keep them from communicating. Free mobile-to-mobile cell minutes and other forms of technology allowed them to speak to each other every single day. Then there were the monthly trips between Atlanta and Detroit.

So how did this long distance love affair remain pure even when they were able to see each other periodically? "When I was in town, I stayed with a friend, and when he would visit me in Atlanta, he stayed at his brother's house. We did it for the sake of accountability. We stayed with people who knew where we were, when we were coming back, and they kept track of us," Nicki Lynch says.

They dated long-distance for a year and a half before they began premarital counseling and were married in 2006.

For more information about their businesses,
visit Moeski and Nicki Lynch at
www.righteousent.com and www.Advbt.com

Keith and JaVon Jason
First Kiss at the Altar

K eith and JaVon met in 1999 at church. Both students at different state colleges, Keith always felt JaVon was attractive however at the time JaVon was in a relationship with someone else so he wasn't able to 'holler at her' right away. JaVon, too, thought Keith was

Keith, 29, and JaVon, 29, with Jozef Jason and Joziah Jason (in the womb) of Ypsilanti, MI

cute and after her relationship ended in 2002, she started seeing him around the church more often.

JaVon recalls one day at church service, she felt the Lord speak to her spirit, as she spotted Keith across the room, "If you ever started dating him, he would be your husband." JaVon kept that experience in her heart, however she couldn't see how it could happen. She didn't think he would like her because she was quiet and she thought he would want someone with an outgoing personality like his. Little did she know he found her very attractive, even more so as he observed her faithfulness and commitment to the ministry and how she conducted herself.

Unbeknownst to them, a mutual friend starting talking to each of them about one another, until finally Keith Jason hung around after JaVon's dance ministry practice and chatted with her until he eventually got invited to her birthday party thrown by a mutual friend. It was there that their friendship would blossom into what eventually turned into a serious dating relationship as they began dating in 2004.

Keith remembers one night having a dream about JaVon. They were getting married and shared their very first kiss at the altar. Upon waking up from that dream, Keith had confirmation not only that JaVon was the one, but he also had direction about how he was going to lead their relationship.

So Keith told JaVon, while driving in the car one day, that he wasn't interested in having a physical relationship with her. He told her they wouldn't kiss until their wedding day, and JaVon's heart rejoiced, especially having come out of a previous relationship which led to nothing but disappointment, heartache and pain.

Keith and JaVon dated and 'stayed saved' by group dating, dating in public places such as the mall or plays, and since they were both at school at the time, they also hung out at the library together.

JaVon appreciated the fact that Keith respected

her and was a true gentleman who opened doors for her and really listened to what she said. "I wanted to show her that chivalry is not dead," Keith recalls. In showing her chivalry was not dead, and in sincerely caring for one another which eventually led to love, Keith and JaVon Jason married in 2006.

Keith and JaVon Jason both work in education.

Esosa and Shereena Osai
Over 50 Years of Virginity Combined

E sosa and Shereena met through family friends. Shereena was friends with one of his sister's best friends and would accompany them to some of Esosa's home fellowships and ministry events as he is a well-known gospel D.J. in the Detroit area.

Esosa remembers, at the age of 21, writing a vision for his life which included a vision for his future wife. He recalls, "It wasn't like, 'she gotta

Esosa, 29, and Shereena, 26, of Detroit, MI

171

be this tall and brown-skinned and all that.' It was just like character issues, gifts and talents that I knew I needed to help me (in what I'm called to do). Of course some attraction as well, so I had written that down and prayed and fasted over it a few years ago."

Well, God honored his prayer request as he met and began observing Shereena. She lined up exactly with what he needed and he was able to observe her fruit and her many gifts and talents.

They began dating and by the second date, Esosa had drawn up a relationship "constitution" of sorts which detailed what their relationship would look like, how affection would be shown, and what to expect. Shereena said, with regards to the constitution, "It gave me a sense of security. I knew that this man wasn't going to be dating me for five years and then change his mind. I knew that he was dating me for the purpose of marriage."

They dated and "stayed saved," by dating in public, hugging, and holding hands. They also dated in groups, were not allowed in each other's bedrooms, and only visited each other's houses if Shereena's parents were home or if his roommates were home. All the boundaries were established up front in the constitution.

Their commitment was consummated on their wedding day as they, both virgins, experienced each other for the first time that night. Shereena says, "Not having sex with each other was a way that we showed love to each other. I loved him enough not to cause him to sin."

*For more information about their business and ministry, visit Esosa Osai at **www.fpdj.com** and Shereena Osai at **www.tes-ti-phy.com***

Eddie and Joanna Willis
Healed and Restored

B y every account, one could conclude that Joanna's heart had not only been bruised, but broken. It had not only been seared, but shattered. On a painful night on her college campus in 2000, Joanna was sexually assaulted.

Joanna, who had been raised in a Christian home, knew that she could not be a successful, saved single person if she did not receive healing

Eddie, 27, and Joanna, 28, of Southfield, MI

from her past. Therefore, two years later, she told a campus ministry counselor who encouraged her to see a professional counselor and the two counselors, along with divine intervention, helped Joanna get healed and restored from what could have been a life-altering experience that may have changed the way she viewed men forever.

However, like Joanna says, "But God."

Five months after her last counseling session, she met Eddie.

Eddie, a young man who was raised in holiness by his parents who, at 14, had promised God he would remain a virgin until marriage, walked inside the coffee shop which was the hang-out spot after their church's singles meeting. Eddie recalls immediately being captivated by Joanna's striking beauty as he stepped inside the shop. He introduced himself to her, sat near and observed her conversation as he decided to order a round of (coffee) drinks on him.

That one night began a yearlong friendship. Eddie and Joanna explained how they purposely did not hang out alone in their friendship stage, but instead spent time together in a group setting to learn and observe each other in a safe and pressure-free environment.

Joanna recalls one day feeling comfortable enough to share her testimony regarding the assault with Eddie. To her surprise, he didn't judge or condemn her, but instead was very compassionate, non-judgmental and shared Scripture with her and encouraged her in the Lord.

As an upcoming author and speaker, Joanna advises young women, "When things happen to you that you cannot control it doesn't mean that you're damaged goods or that you can't be married because that's what satan wants you to believe--because you feel stained or that no one will want you anymore--but instead you want to be with someone who's going to help cultivate you, lift you up and remind you of your restoration. "

"God prepared me for this," Eddie says. "I was raised to be a husband. I wanted to be married since I was a teenager." Eddie believed God for a wife who had a servant's heart like he does and he was able to observe that in his future wife.

Their year-long friendship turned into a year-long dating relationship then a year-long engagement. For three years, Eddie and Joanna remained abstinent until marriage.

When asked, "How did you do it?" Eddie responded, "I made sure to put the 'fail-safes' in our relationship." He had spelled out on paper what he couldn't handle, what he wrestled with in the flesh, and they were completely honest with each other. Some of the rules included not dating each other late at night. If they were in a home, either of their parents were home, who were also their accountability partners.

Eddie and Joanna were married in 2008 and have

been experiencing true happiness and marital bliss ever since.

*Eddie Willis is a real estate agent, counselor, property manager, and singer. Joanna Willis is an upcoming Christian author of the book, **But God**, and is also a social worker supervisor, and a Limited License Counselor, LLPC*

Clarence and Rolisia Siebert
Write the Vision

Clarence, 30, and Rolisia, 28, of Garden City, MI

Clarence and Rolisia met each other while serving together at church – Clarence as a new usher and Rolisia as a new hostess. Initially shocked that two "newbies" were placed to serve together side by side, Rolisia recalls noticing, "something different about him," upon meeting him. Clarence admits that he was initially attracted to her, but more than anything he was drawn to her quality of character and her warm personality.

He eventually approached Rolisia to date her and was told he had to first meet with her father before going out. He did, and Rolisia admits that Clarence was the first man that her father approved of and that her father, whom she described as a "man's man," even cried. It was then that Clarence, who had rededicated his life back to Christ in 2000, three years prior to dating her, knew that Rolisia wasn't just any girl, but that she was special and that he was accountable not only to her but also to her father, which caused Clarence to respect and cherish his find even more.

Before they officially started dating, they comprised a Commitment Letter which stated the boundaries which wouldn't be crossed or what was allowed during their relationship. For example, it mentioned their dating curfew for weekends and during the week, no sitting between each other's legs, no watching certain TV programs, and no idle time. They shared this letter with Rolisia's father, Clarence's mother, and with a married couple they were accountable to at the time. Clarence says, "We used Numbers 30:2 as our foundation Scripture – it was our commitment to honor our relationship and honor God."

Clarence and Rolisia dated almost three years before they married in 2006.

Clarence advises couples to, "Represent." (for God) Be the first to lead the way (as far as abstinence until marriage) and set the new standard because you have folks watching you that you don't realize they're watching you."

Rolisia advises single women: "Know what you want. I declared to God that I didn't have time to waste. When you date, date with a purpose knowing you're worth more than just dating to 'hang out and pass time.' I told God, 'I'm willing to wait forever for the right one.' I had been hurt so bad in the past that I just fell into God's arms and He restored me and He promised me that if I followed Him, I wouldn't have to hurt like that again. So know what you want, be vocal about what you want, and set your expectation up front and if he's the right one, then he will respect that."

Clarence Siebert is a production worker who also specializes in Home Improvements with his business, Project Jesus.
Rolisia Siebert is a licensed professional counselor specializing in therapy for children, teens, families, and women's issues.

Dexter and Tiffany Godfrey
From Bible Study to Bah Dum Pa Dum

D exter and Tiffany met each other while attending the same church in 1995.

Dexter often observed Tiffany as she assisted and served in various church activities such as the choir and the single's ministry. A year later, they started dating after teaching vacation Bible study together.

They dated for three and a half years and Dexter admits that she was his first relationship in which he remained faithful and Tiffany says he was her first relationship after she got saved at 21. Tiffany fell in love with Dexter's sincere love for the Lord and how he makes her laugh just like her father does.

Dexter and Tiffany dated and "stayed saved" by preparing Bible

Dexter, 39, and Tiffany, 35, of Hampton, VA

study lessons together, and remaining active and occupied while serving in different auxiliaries at their church. Tiffany also mentioned that while she dated Dexter, she lived with an elderly lady who was sort of a chaperone whose home she didn't want to disrespect by fooling around with "some man" in her house.

Though Dexter admits to being sexually active before Tiffany, once he started dating her, he made the decision to take sex out of the equation. He said, "I didn't want to do anything to cloud my decision because for me marriage is forever so I took marriage very seriously and sleeping with women could have clouded my thought process. I wanted to do this relationship completely different."

He also said he didn't want to ruin his testimony since he worked with the youth and was very much active in church.

Dexter and Tiffany now have a bouncing boy, HJ, and have been married 10 years at the writing of this book. They recently celebrated their 10-year anniversary on a Caribbean cruise.

Dexter advises Christian couples: "Find out each other's future goals and make sure they're compatible – find out what else you have in common besides Jesus."

Tiffany encourages women: "Know your identity in Christ and allow what Christ says about you to override what your past says about you...Love yourself, don't lower your standards, and don't settle.

Pray for discernment while dating because you want to make sure the person you're dating is the one for you."

Dexter would like to tell single men that finding your wife is a marathon, and not a sprint. He says, "Before you go out and seek your wife, seek your purpose – look beyond the physical, look also for substance and listen to God in regards to who is the right woman for you."

Dexter is a real estate trainer and investor.
Tiffany is a writer and relationship expert.

Mike and Lisa Gordon
Worth the Wait

When Mike first met Lisa in 2000 at a church sponsored get-a-way retreat for college-age students, he immediately knew that there was something special about her that wasn't just physical - but something different. "She was a light in the room. She stood out to me a lot," he recalls. He then prayed about and observed her without Lisa's knowledge over the next year and inquired about her to people who knew her. After he received what he described as a 'green light' of peace from God, He eventually approached her to date her.

Since Lisa was away at college during most of their courtship, they spent a lot of time talking on the phone - learning as much about one another as possible. Lisa, who was a virgin, told Mike up front that she wasn't going to have sex with him because

Lisa, 29, Mike, 31, and sons
(l to r) Andre Josiah and Mike II
of Lathrup Village, MI

her mother taught her as a child to save herself. Mike already knew he wasn't going to have sex with Lisa because he had learned from past relationships years prior that premarital sex was no longer an option for him. He told Lisa she was worth the wait.

Mike and Lisa carried out their commitment to God and one another by dating in public places such as the mall, hanging out with other couples, or if she stopped by his house, his parents or family members would always be present and they didn't date each other late at night. "We didn't trust our flesh," Mike said.

Once they were engaged, they both admitted to being more challenged in the flesh because of their sheer desire for one another, but they carried out their commitment until marriage in 2003 and had their first son, Mike Gordon II, in 2007 and second son, Andre Josiah Gordon, in 2008.

When asked what advice do you have for a single man who is believing God for a mate, Mike says, "Be happy single, first, and not in a rush. Learn how to be at peace with and appreciate your singleness. Learn how to spend your money and budget as a single person."

Lisa encourages single women to, "Know who you are in God and how He sees you as valuable and precious and truly internalize that." She also encourages women not to chase after or 'position' themselves in a certain man's pathway. "Get out of his face," she says. "You do not need to position yourself in front of a man. Like the saying goes, 'you should be so hidden in God that the man has to seek God in order to find you.' You are worth the wait."

Mike Gordon is a realtor with Keller Williams Realty.
*For more information visit **www.GordonHomes1.com***
Lisa Gordon is a stay-at-home mom.

FINAL WORDS OF ENCOURAGEMENT

I t is my sincere desire that this book blessed you in a major way and allowed you to see God's perfect will and heartbeat when it comes to dating relationships and marriage. A decision to remain abstinent until marriage pleases God, and as single believers our number one aim should be to please Him. He is our Master, He is our Savior, and He is our Lord and He desires to be Lord over our lives and over everything we do. He loves us so much that He sent His Son, Jesus, from heaven, who was living it up in glory, down to this green earth for the sole purpose of dying for each and every one of our sins, including the sin of fornication, or sexual relations outside of marriage. Jesus died for that sin, not so we can return to it again, but so that we can walk in newness of life and be restored and become the best God would have us to be.

Remaining abstinent until marriage is not about the act alone. Jesus died for the "act" and we thank God for His blood in that if we sincerely confess our sin, He cleanses us and puts us right back in right standing with God. But what a sinful lifestyle does is it slows the hand of God in relation to the purpose, plan, and path that He has for each of our lives.

For example, it took the children of Israel 40 years to get to the promised land, a place where biblical scholars say it should have only taken them a few days. But because of their sins of idol worship, rebellion, and because of their grumbling and complaining all the time which are sins as well (Philippians 2:14, 1 Thessalonians 5:18), it took them longer to receive the blessing God had in store for them.

When we live a lifestyle of sexual sin, outside of the will of God, we stop God from blessing us, operating in our lives, and leading us into His perfect will for our lives and our own individual destinies. God's thoughts towards us are peace and not of evil to give us an expected end and hope in our final outcome (Jeremiah 29:11). The path that He has laid out for us is as the shining light which shines more and more unto the perfect day (Proverbs 4:18).

It is not until we settle this issue and live abstinent and holy before God as single believers that God can then elevate and promote us to our next level in Him.

His dream and His desire is to prosper you and make your name great. He wants you to be the best because He is your Creator and He is that loving

Father who wants to see His child do well and excel in life. He wants to use you, and He wants you to be blessed and a major blessing to all those you encounter. He wants to lead and guide you to that land that flows with milk and honey for your life. When we operate in sexual sin as single believers, we are operating in short-sightedness. Because we don't see the big picture of what God has for our lives, we settle for the small pleasures of sin which can ruin and destroy our lives and our destinies.

Know that your decision to remain abstinent until marriage, from this day forth, is sowing seed into your destiny. You're sowing seed into your breakthrough. And, more than anything, you're telling God, "Thank you," for the sacrifice that He made for you, and the price that He paid for you, which was the shed blood of Jesus Christ.

Single believer, may God continue to strengthen and encourage your heart. If you're not dating right now, focus on pleasing God, serve in your local church, and be a blessing to your friends and family, while knowing that all the promises of God in Him are always, yea and amen, and that what God has for you, is for you, in His season for your life. Enjoy the journey!

Much love in Christ,

Kim Brooks

IN-PUBLIC DATING IDEAS FOR CHRISTIAN COUPLES

A trip to the zoo
Amusement Park
Apple Orchard
Attend a seminar together
Boat ride
Bowling
Breakfast
Brunch
Canoing
Carnivals, festivals, and other outdoor shows
Church sponsored event (i.e. church play, dinner)
Coffee Shop
Cooking Class
Dance lessons (i.e. ballroom, gospel hustle)
Downtown festivals and attractions
Go out for ice cream
Go-Kart Racing
Gospel concert

Have a picnic at a playground
Hayride
Historic Places and Buildings
Horseback riding with a group
Hot Air Balloon Ride
Sky Diving
Ice Skating
Karaoke
Laser Tag
Museum (sometimes they offer pottery lessons
   or free painting classes)
Opera
Paintball
Parasailing
Plane ride
Play
Play Date
Putt-Putt golfing
Rent a fancy car and drive out of state
   (great opportunity to communicate and
   travel at the same time)
Roller Skating
Skydiving
Sporting events
Trip to the circus with your nieces or nephews
Trip to the zoo
Video Arcade
Volunteer together at a soup kitchen
   or homeless shelter
Whirleyball

Prayer of Salvation

I f you read this book and you have never received Jesus Christ as your personal Lord and
Savior, I would like to invite you to make the
best decision you could ever make in your entire
life!

Romans 10:9-10 states:

That if thou shall confess with thy mouth the Lord Jesus,
and shalt believe in thine heart that God hath raised
him from the dead, thou shalt be saved. For with the
heart man believeth unto righteousness; and with the
mouth confession is made unto salvation.

Recite this prayer out loud:

"Father, God, I believe that Jesus Christ is the Son
of God. I believe He died for me, carried my sins
for me, and that He arose, and is alive right now.
Lord, Jesus, come into my heart. I repent of sin,
and I turn toward You. I receive You as my Savior,
and I confess You as my Lord. I thank You, Lord,
that according to Your Word, I am born again. In
Jesus' Name, Amen."

Praise God, you are saved! Though you still look
the same on the outside, on the inside you are a
new creature in Christ according to 2 Corinthians
5:17.

If you do not have a church home, I encourage you to join and become active in one that teaches the Word of God so that you will continue to grow spiritually. When it comes to choosing a church home, go where you grow!

Today marks a day of new beginnings for you! Sign and date below as a way to remember this day forever.

Signature _____

Date _____

REDEDICATION

If you have read this book and are saved, but have since fallen away from God, or are out of fellowship with God and want to come back to Him, then recite this prayer:

"Father God, please forgive me for I have sinned. Your Word says that if I confess my sins than you are faithful and just to forgive me of my sins and cleans me of all unrighteousness. Please forgive me for (state the sins), and also any place in my heart where I have missed the mark. Thank You for honoring Your Word and bringing me back in right standing with You as I have confessed my sin, with the heart intention of not doing it again. Thank You for the shed blood of Jesus which has washed away my sin and has brought me back in right standing with You as I continue and strive to be the godly person You have called and pre-destined me to be. In Jesus' Name, Amen."

Praise God, you are cleansed of sin! You are whole! You are back in right standing with God. You can now feel free to praise and worshop God freely, lifting up holy hands without wrath or doubting. Remember, if you ever miss the mark, always run to God, never away from God, and He'll be standing right there with opened arms, ready to receive you once again.

Signature _____

Date _____

Abstinence until Marriage Pledge

"Father God, in the Name of Jesus, this day I commit to glorifying You with my body, soul, and spirit. I offer my body as a living sacrifice, and I pledge to commit to abstinence until marriage which is my reasonable service.

I recognize that at times I may feel tempted or weak, but it's in these times that I will seek strength and guidance from You and Your Word. I can do nothing in and of myself, however I can do all things through Christ who strengthens me, including from henceforth abstaining from sex until marriage. In Jesus' Name, Amen."

Signature _____

Date _____

*Tear out this page and post it on your bedroom wall or keep it tucked inside your Bible as a way to remember your commitment to God. From this day forward, you are worth the wait, and you can do it!

*Email me your testimony or commitment pledge through my website www.DateandStaySaved.com

ABOUT THE AUTHOR

Award-winning author, licensed minister, national speaker and songwriter, **Kim Brooks,** of Detroit, MI is the Black Expressions Bestselling Author of, *He's Fine...But is He Saved?* its Black Christian Book Distributors Bestselling sequel, *He's Saved...But is He For Real?* and highly acclaimed non-fiction debut, *The Little Black Survival Book for Single Saints.*

She is an honors graduate of Word of Faith Bible Training Center, and an English graduate of Michigan State University.

An abstinence until marriage advocate, which is not only her speaking platform but also her testimony as she is a virgin in her early thirties, Kim has been featured in *Gospel Today, JET, The Detroit News,* and has appeared as a guest on *The Word Network, Totally Christian Television,* and *Christian Television Network.*

Her ministry and message is spread throughout her books, blogs, songs, articles and poems and has been heard on airwaves nationwide including *Rhythm and Praise* with Pastor Marvin L. Winans, *Strong Inspirations* with Dr. Deborah Smith Pollard, *The Praise Party* with Ace Alexander, *Rejoice Musical Soulfood,* and many others. As the President of Driven Enterprises, LLC and founder of Driven Heart Ministries, she is also a contributing columnist for *Hope for Women Magazine and Masterpiece Magazine.*

Kim Brooks' powerful message, which brings hope and healing to the nation, is that it *is possible* to live an exciting, uncompromising, drama-free, purpose-driven, Spirit-led, victorious life in the perfect will of God!

To contact Kim, or to receive a free gift for signing-up to receive her free monthly eNewsletter for singles entitled, *The Single Heart,* visit ***www.DateandStaySaved.com***
Join the movement!

Book a ***How To Date and Stay Saved Workshop*** for your next singles conference or youth explosion,
or invite Kim to minister at your next event.

Send an invitation letter to:
Kim Brooks, PO Box 231856, Detroit, MI 48223

or Email: booking@dateandstaysaved.com

or Call: 1-313-541-2856

I f this book blessed you, tell a single friend, or buy a loved one his or her very own copy as this book will be referenced continuously throughout one's dating experiences up until marriage.

How To Date and Stay Saved is available in bookstores nationwide, Amazon.com, or you can receive a personalized, discounted auto-graphed copy by ordering through **www.DateandStaySaved.com** (all major credit cards accepted) or by completing this order form and enclosing a check or money order.

	Price	Qty	$ Total
How to Date & Stay Saved	$12.95		

+Shipping/Handling $4.95 (add $2.00 for each additional book)

Name:_____

Address: _____

City/State: _____

Zip Code: _____

Phone: _____

Email: _____

Name you would like inscribed in the book(s):

_____

_____

Make Check or Money Order Payable To: **Driven Enterprises**
*Allow 3-5 business days for delivery upon receipt of payment.
For check or money order, please complete the order form, tear it out and mail to:

Driven Enterprises
P.O. Box 231856 • Detroit, MI 48223
Tel: 1-313-541-2856
Reading group questions and group/bulk order discounts for
singles ministries, book clubs, organizations, or other groups can
be found on www.DateAndStaySaved.com

OTHER BOOKS BY KIM BROOKS

Fiction
He's Fine...But is He Saved?
(Kimani Press/Harlequin)

He's Saved...But is He For Real?
(Kimani Press/Harlequin)

Non-fiction
**The Little Black Survival Book
For Single Saints**
(Driven Enterprises)

Acknowledgements

Where do I begin? God has been so faithful, so I must start with Him. Thank you, Lord, for birthing yet another book through me. Words cannot describe my love for You; I pray this book truly blesses and encourages Your people.

I would also like to thank my family, who has been so supportive since I read my first poem to classmates in elementary school. No matter the occasion, recital or event, you were there for me then, and continue to be there for me now. Many thanks to my mom, Lutricia Brooks, my dad, Lawrence Brooks, my stepmom, Wallein, my sister, Kelley, my nephew (future world-shaker) Sean, my uncle and aunt, Owsley and Henrietta Spiller, my Uncle John, and my cousins Donna and Karen. Many thanks also to my family down south and beyond. I love you!

Special thanks to my pastor, Bishop Keith A. Butler of Word of Faith International Christian Center. For the past 14 years, you have taught me the unadulterated Word of God and you were the first to teach me about pursuing my purpose. Thank you also, First Family, and my entire Word of Faith family.

Many thanks to my "team" who helped bring this project to pass: My editor, Skyla Thomas of Pleasant Words, LLC and my book cover and interior layout designer, LaTanya Orr of iSelah, LLC. Dynamic Duo!

Thank you to the following for their mentorship and continued support: Jacquelin Thomas, Tia McCollors, Kendra Norman-Bellamy, Christine Pembleton, Dr. Deborah Smith Pollard, Dr. Kenya Ayers, Ed Houston, Larry W. Robinson, Carol Mackey, Kim "Kiwi" Williams, Stephanie L. Jones, Ed Gray, Jillian Blackwell, Jessica Y. Hernandez, Pastor Lori Nichols, Evangelist Marie Diggs, Minister Burdette, and Ellis Liddell.

Many thanks to the married couples featured in the final chapter who openly and willingly shared their testimonies of how they dated their spouses and "stayed saved" until after they said, "I do."

(Big Hug) Thanks to all media who have supported me and continue to support me over the years including radio, TV, magazines, online media and periodicals. Thank you for allowing my voice and platform to be heard. A special thanks to all the bookstores and libraries who have carried my books.

(God Bless You) Thank you to the best publicist/pr coach in the biz - Pam Perry, of Ministry Marketing Solutions, for encouraging me to follow my dreams even when I felt like giving up.

And last, but not least, I'd like to thank my readers for all their encouraging words and support. May the Lord bless you with all the desires of your heart, as you seek His face and delight in Him! *(Psalm 37:4)*

CPSIA information can be obtained at www.ICGtesting.com
Printed in the USA
BVOW04s1919100215

387179BV00003B/9/P